The CRUCIFIXION *of* MINISTRY

Surrendering Our Ambitions to the Service of Christ

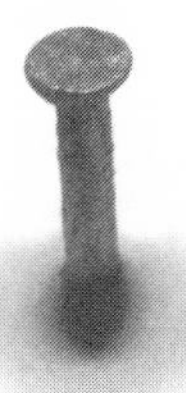

ANDREW PURVES

An imprint of InterVarsity Press
Downers Grove, Illinois

InterVarsity Press
P.O. Box 1400, Downers Grove, IL 60515-1426
World Wide Web: www.ivpress.com
E-mail: email@ivpress.com

InterVarsity Press® is the book-publishing division of InterVarsity Christian Fellowship/USA®, a student movement active on campus at hundreds of universities, colleges and schools of nursing in the United States of America, and a member movement of the International Fellowship of Evangelical Students. For information about local and regional activities, write Public Relations Dept., InterVarsity Christian Fellowship/USA, 6400 Schroeder Rd., P.O. Box 7895, Madison, WI 53707-7895, or visit the IVCF website at <www.intervarsity.org>.

Design: Cindy Kiple
Images: José Carlos Pires Pereira/iStockphoto

ISBN 978-0-8308-3439-6

Printed in the United States of America ∞

Library of Congress Cataloging-in-Publication Data

Purves, Andrew, 1946-
The crucifixion of ministry: surrendering our ambitions to the service of Christ / Andrew Purves.
p. cm.
Includes bibliographical references and index.
ISBN 978-0-8308-3439-6 (pbk.: alk. paper)
1. Church work. 2. Pastoral theology. 3. Jesus Christ—Example.
I. Title.
BV4400.P87 2007
253—dc22

2007021568

P 19 18 17 16 15 14 13 12 11 10 9 8 7 6 5 4 3 2 1
Y 23 22 21 20 19 18 17 16 15 14 13 12 11 10 09 08 07

Dedicated with respect to the courageous men and women who know something of the crucifixion of their ministries and yet keep the faith.

And with love to Cathy, as always a wonderful wife, a terrific friend and a faithful minister of Jesus Christ, who knows the pain and the hope of the crucifixion of ministry.

Contents

PREFACE

MY WIFE, CATHY, AND I WERE WALKING on the beach at the end of our vacation. We were musing on our imminent return to work, she to her congregation where she is minister, I to the seminary where I teach. She especially was struggling with the issues of ministry. Among a range of emotions she expressed frustration that no matter what she tried, nothing much seemed to change.

Suddenly, I mean out of the blue, I had the insight that there is little, maybe nothing, we who are ministers of the gospel can do that really changes things. If anything worthwhile is to happen, Jesus has to show up.

The insight was simple; yet it was very significant, even radical. By trade I am a pastoral theologian. I am supposed to know about the theory and theology of ministry. That moment on the beach marked my realization that our ministries themselves are not redemptive. Only the ministry of Jesus is redemptive.

As a professional theologian I sit on the sidelines and observe. I think, I teach and I write. Yet I have learned much from living with a wife who day in and day out works through the frustrations and the joys of ministry. Ministers can't forgive sinners, raise the dead or bring in the kingdom of God. Neither can we grow congregations, convert sinners or heal the dying. Cathy's pain has taught me that Jesus has to show up and do what he has promised to do.

Walking on the beach I was suddenly aware that our attempt to be effective ministers is a major problem. We are in the way. Our strategies, action plans, pastoral resources and entrepreneurial church revitalization techniques have become not the solution but the problem. Our ministries need to be crucified. They need to be killed off.

What if Jesus showed up? That's our only hope. Our people don't need us; they need Jesus. Our job is to bear witness to him, trusting that he continues to be the One who forgives, blesses, heals, renews, instructs and bring life out of death.

This book reworks some of the ground covered in my *Reconstructing Pastoral Theology: A Christological Foundation* (Westminster John Knox, 2004), though in a nontechnical manner. It also includes entirely new material. I have pushed my thinking far beyond the conclusions of my last book as I have developed the idea of the crucifixion of ministry and as I have outlined the structure of pastoral ministry as bearing witness, interpretation and symbolic action.

My thanks go out to the ministers in various groups and conferences where I spoke over the last couple of years. They told me I was on to something. Working with them is a great blessing for me. To students at Pittsburgh Theological Seminary who have sat in my classes and encouraged me—thank you. And finally, thanks to a terrific company of faculty colleagues. What a privilege to be part of something amazing that God is doing among us.

INTRODUCTION

Has God Killed Your Ministry Yet?

THE CRUCIFIXION OF MINISTRY IS GOOD NEWS! My goal in this book is to offer a perspective on ministry and illustrate a practice that liberates ministers from the grind of feeling that "it's all up to me." I have two themes:

1. Conceiving ministry as *our* ministry is the root problem of what ails us in ministry today.
2. Ministry should be understood as a sharing in the continuing ministry of Jesus Christ, for wherever Christ is, there is the church and her ministry.

I intend for my writing to be readily accessible to busy, tired, somewhat depressed, midcareer and fed-up ministers who can't carry the load of ministry any longer. I hope that some selfstyled successful ministers will also read it and find a wholly new way to be in ministry.

WHAT GOD IS UP TO

I begin where ministry must always begin, with the practice of God. By that I mean *what God is up to*. The practice of God is not an easy concept. The most important point is this: God is an actor in our present experience. We would not know God otherwise. Do I believe that Jesus is the living, reigning and acting Lord? Everything hinges on a positive answer.

The question involves an *either-or.* Here is the *either:* If Jesus is properly understood to be nothing more than a continuing moral influence, then it is up to us to actualize and achieve everything in faith, life and ministry. Jesus becomes powerless and is of little help. Like a fossil trapped in amber, Jesus is locked into an abstract and theoretical theological system. He is an idea which we must somehow incarnate as best we can to make him and his cause effective today. Having given us a moral code and ministerial imperatives, he now sits on the sidelines of the cosmos, arms folded, waiting for us to do something. The best we can hope for is a cheerleader Christ. He cheers us on when we do well, but he is not involved in the game.

Get Jesus wrong by consigning him to be only metaphorically alive as a continuing moral influence, and what is left? A ministry experience that inevitably bounces between guilt and burnout. We labor under the weight of the ministerial imperative: *do it.* But we soon discover we can't do it at all.

Now here is the *or:* Jesus is God active in the life of the world, in our personal lives and in ministry at every turn. The issue is not *How does Jesus get in on our ministries?* Instead, because he is the living and reigning Lord, the issue is now *What is he up to, and how do I hitch a ride on whatever he is up to?*

Where Christ Is, There Is the Church

We find the answers in the classical Christian doctrines of our participation through union with Christ in his vicarious humanity and ministry. Everything is cast back on to him, onto God who is present for us by the Spirit, onto Jesus Christ who is the same yesterday, today and forever. Because ministry is what Jesus does, ministry is properly understood as gospel rather than law and as grace rather than obligation.

The first and central question in thinking about ministry is *Who is Jesus Christ and what is he up to?* The answer leads to the second question: *How do we get in on Jesus' ministry?* This is my way of restating a very old doctrine. It is thought to have been stated first by Ignatius of Antioch from the end of the first Christian century at the close of the apostolic age: *Where Christ is, there is the church* (*ubi Christus, ibi ecclesia*). We can also mimic how the twentieth century Swiss theologian Karl Barth said it: *It is not Jesus Christ who needs our ministries; it is our ministries that need Jesus Christ.* So my dictum is *Wherever Christ is present in ministry, there my ministry may be found.* It is the implication for ministry in Jesus' words, "Apart from me you can do nothing" (John 15:5).

Displaced Ministry

Exploring these issues will bring us to the difficult awareness that our ministries must be displaced by the ministry of Jesus. Displacement is more than relinquishment. Displacement is not an invitation to let Jesus take over by letting him in on our territory. Rather, we must be bumped aside firmly, perhaps mortifyingly. Otherwise we will never let go of our grip on our ministries. We are too attached to them and to their payoff, even if at times the payoff is negative.

Displacement literally means the death of our ministries. All that we think we *should* do and *can* do and *are doing* in ministry must be put to death. Why? Because too often our ministries are in the way. Even when we conduct them from the best spiritual, therapeutic and moral motives, they are not redemptive. Only the ministry of Jesus is redemptive.

Crucifixion: Good News

I call the process of displacement "the crucifixion of ministry" because in Christian thought crucifixion carries the concept of redemption. The crucifixion of Jesus is staggering good news of our salvation. The crucifixion of ministry by the process of painful displacement by the ministry of Jesus is staggering good news for ministers and for the people among whom we minister. The crucifixion of ministry is the ground for the redemption of our ministries. For us, the ministers, it is the source of hope, joy and peace in our service.

None of this should come as a surprise. Jesus told us to take up our cross daily—to die daily—and follow him (Luke 9:23). Paul writes of being crucified with Christ (Galatians 2:19). Why would our ministries not be included in that crucifixion?

The Christian theology of baptism reminds us that as we have died with Christ, so also we will be raised with Christ (Romans 6:4; Colossians 2:12). Paul sums up all Christian living this way: "You have died, and your life is hidden with Christ in God" (Colossians 3:3). We should expect that our ministries too should die, even be killed, that they may be raised with Christ.

YOU JUST NAILED ME!

When I speak at conferences about the crucifixion of ministry, ministers often approach me afterward and say, "You just nailed me!" It is an especially appropriate response to the idea of the crucifixion of ministry! I find, however, that seminary students rarely internalize and appropriate the lesson of the crucifixion of ministry and the theology behind it. Perhaps we have to be bashed about in ministry for a while before we learn that the crucifixion of ministry is God's gift.

The theology of the vicarious humanity and ministry of Christ, which is the theological foundation for much of my argument, is not difficult to grasp at a cognitive level, but it is difficult to internalize so that it begins to deeply and redemptively form our ministry. A former Doctor of Ministry student wrote to me that "I find it easy to talk a good game about how Christ is the one sanctifying us, but more often than I care to admit, in practice I minister like a Pelagian." The truth of Christ in our stead must convert us in heart and mind, seeping deeply into our ministerial souls, until it reorders our homiletical and pastoral practice according to the ministry of the living, acting and reigning Lord Jesus.

A Dull Christmas Eve

Cathy, my wife, is minister of a small urban Presbyterian congregation in Pittsburgh, Pennsylvania. I was sitting with my adult children during a moderately dull Christmas Eve service. The attendance was rather poor. The choir seemed a bit off and unenergetic. At the beginning of the sermon a couple of under-fives got free from their parents and began to noisily roam the pews, which was charming but made it hard to concentrate on what Cathy was saying.

Later that night I confessed to Cathy that I had really struggled with my annoyance at small congregations. I recall thinking, "I bet my friend Craig Barnes at Shadyside [a large, prosperous city congregation] is putting on a great show tonight." Then a truth dawned on me! I had spent part of the day writing this chapter, and in the evening I had already forgotten what I had written.

I came into the Christmas Eve service demanding excellence in musical and homiletical performance. My attitude was *What will they do to give me a Christmas Eve spiritual high?* With a prideful sense of entitlement I had focused on the ministry of the musicians and the preacher. I realized with sadness that I had looked at the finger rather than at what the finger was pointing to, the ministry of God with and for us. The service was not about the choir's performance, the quality of the sermon (which actually was very good) or the meditative calm of the sanctuary. It was about the celebration of the birth of Emmanuel, who in the Spirit was present there with us. And I had missed it!

Christ's Ministry in Our Place

We have to move away from thinking about ministry and all its attendant strategies, programs and processes, and think rather of Christ's ministry in our place and what it means that we are connected to him. The form and content of our ministry will then take an explicitly christological content and shape. The change is hard for us because it means that ministry is no longer about us and our skills. It is now about the *real presence* of Jesus Christ, whenever and wherever in his gracious freedom and love he is Emmanuel, God *with* us. The actuality of his ministry is what makes our ministry possible.

Today we are living and serving through a very difficult time. It is difficult because of the decline of the huge intellectual experiment called the Enlightenment, the emergence of postmodernity and the breakdown of all the great systems of thought that characterized the modern age. In that context my goal is to affirm and explore for the practice of ministry the radically converting truth spoken by John the Baptist, "He [Jesus] must increase, but I must decrease" (John 3:30).

Clergy Burnout

What is happening to us, we who are the ministers of Jesus Christ? Many of us are professionally, spiritually and financially depressed. The figures produced by studies only serve to quantify what we have bitterly experienced for ourselves. Something is very wrong, and the costs—personal, spiritual, familial and financial, as well as congregational—are terrifying.

For example, one respected study concluded that around 40 percent of Lutheran Church—Missouri Synod clergy suffer from mild to severe burnout. From my experience teaching doctor of ministry students for a quarter of a century, I believe the same experience is common across all denominations. Our stress levels are at a medically significant level. Denominational health insurance agencies report that medical costs for clergy are higher than for any other professional group!

Another report, a summary of which was written by Michael Jinkins of Austin Theological Seminary and published by the respected Alban Institute in 2002, is poignantly titled "Great Expectations: Sobering Realities." Of the study's sample group, 62 percent of ministers have little spiritual life! Excessive demands on time, conflicts within congregations and between ministers and members, loss of personal spiritual life and loneliness account for a deep malaise within our professional and personal lives.

Each of the following stories is true, although appropriately disguised. Jack, a nationally known minister in a prestigious suburban congregation, told me that although it never actually happened, he could hear in his mind the heavy steps of the personnel committee marching down the hall to his office to tell him it's time to go. Paranoid? Maybe. But it led to an unhappy, anxious ministry. Then there is Jean, my former student, who came weeping to my front door one evening, unable to take any longer the relentless refusal of the leaders of her small rural congregation to participate in any kind of Christian formation and education. "They want a chaplain, not a minister," she complained to me. Bob's ministry is nearly hamstrung over issues between him and a leading family in his congregation concerning war with Iraq, the national flag in the sanctuary and on church grounds, "God Bless America" days (even Mother's Day!) and the congregation's right to sing national songs. There is Tony, who can't cope with the stress of a wife with severe diabetes, three young children and a salary which does not enable him to pay off his $40,000 college and seminary debt. Finally there is Mary, reduced to quivering anxiety over the local denominational pressure to "go missional," leading to worship wars in her congregation and terrific conflict with the choir and organist. She feels that the word from denominational authorities is "grow your congregation or you're out." In an area where new paradigm congregations have exploding memberships, Mary feels depressed and anxious. She feels like a failure, with plummeting confidence in the capacity of the faithful exercise of Word and sacraments to deliver the results demanded.

THEOLOGY WARS

Then there is war on the larger front. Theological debates and denominational politics often display levels of intensifying toxicity that mirror the style and tone of national politics. Organized theological caucuses within denominations significantly drain ministerial energies. There is nowhere to hide from the battles over homosexuality and ordination, inclusive language, the Trinity, Christology, missional or justice agendas, contemporary or traditional worship and so on. So-called mainline pastors minister in the midst of doubt that the major denominations will hold together much longer. All sense of a shared history and a common theological and worship identity are breaking down. For many ministers, the trend of declining membership hits home at the congregational level with an accompanying sense of failure.

Ministry is just not much fun anymore. Of course ministry has always been difficult. Weariness is par for the course. Spiritual embattlement is to be expected. We are not in it for the money. The social status of ministers is low and likely to remain so. I am told that on one sociologist's ranking we are just below a factory foreman. That may not be so bad, but we once held professional status equal to the professions of law and medicine. We are tired, often overworked, usually overstressed and underpaid, theologically confused, often ill-educated for the tasks before us, bored and probably guilty for feeling that way.

Whatever the reasons, national figures show that around one-third of ordained persons leave the ministry after five years, never to return.

It's that bad! The rest of us continue to drag ourselves out of bed in the morning and labor on.

Flawed Education

While I recognize the danger of sweeping generalizations, it appears that something has gone very wrong in the education, nurture and employment expectations of ministers. Those of us in theological education go round and round discussing what to do about it. Year after year we hear the stories of pain from our Doctor of Ministry students. Candor insists that we have been and are part of the problem, just as we must be part of the solution.

I believe that a broadly liberal theology, especially the dilution of classical Christology and decreased interest in the Christian doctrine of the Trinity, have produced a couple of generations of ministers with a theology that fails at the congregational level. The theologians in mainline seminaries have swallowed the bait of accommodation to the dictates of Enlightenment philosophies. The Enlightenment project is now in serious and hopefully terminal decline. As a result, the theological generations who hitched their wagons to its engine are now in disarray.

"Theological reductionism" is a term which means reducing God to fit modern predetermined human categories of experience or rationality. It sometimes known as *foundationalism*. By either name it does not grow congregations or lead to fulfillment in ministry. Read John Hick's book *The Metaphor of God Incarnate: Christology in a Pluralist Age* (Westminster John Knox, 2005), and then ask yourself if this is your hope in ministry and your hope for your congregation.

Bumper Sticker Truth

Now I come to tell you what you already know and prayerfully trust to be true. *Jesus is the answer.* The bumper sticker had it right all along, although I want to spend the rest of this book exploring exactly what it means for ministry.

I believe there is a theological answer for our malaise and disappointment in ministry. The answer has to do with our understanding of God and how we connect to whatever God is up to. My concern is not with complex academic concepts and arguments but with the real and actual practice of God. If theology is *talk about God,* I will not be content to only talk *about* talk about God. I want to dare *to talk about God.* I will put into words what I think God is up to and what it means for our ministries when we share in the actions of God.

A Summary

1. The ministry of Jesus is the ministry of God. That is what most of our creedal and confessional language concerning Jesus Christ is about.
2. Jesus' ministry is not merely a past influence that reaches into the present. It is at once historical, present and future.
3. Wherever Christ is, there is the church. By sharing in the life of Jesus, we thereby share in God's continuing ministry. This is the doctrine of our union with Christ, which is the principal work of the Holy Spirit. It is Christ, not we, who does the ministry.

In what follows I will develop the doctrines of the vicarious humanity and ministry of Jesus and show their significance for us as ministers of the gospel. Then I will look at an approach to ministry characterized as *participation in Christ.* When we understand ministry in this ancient way, we will find Jesus' words true, "My yoke is easy, and my burden is light" (Matthew 11:30).

An Ongoing Crucifixion

Now a word about the book's title, for it tells much about the journey we are about to take. The accounts given above of experiences in ministry amount to a kind of ongoing crucifixion. Ministry kills us with regard to our ego needs, desire for power and success and the persistent wish to feel competent and in control.

It does not take us long to discover that we cannot heal the sick, raise the dead, calm the demonized, guide the morally afflicted, sober up the alcoholic, make the wife beater loving, calm the anxious, pacify the conflicted, control the intemperate, have answers to all the "Why?" questions, give the teenagers a moral compass and preach magnificent sermons every week, all the while growing the congregation and keeping the members happy. We preach and teach, do the round of pastoral visitations and administer the congregation's life, while the soreheads more often than not remain soreheaded, the stubborn remain stubborn, the quarrelsome remain quarrelsome and the stupid seem to get no wiser. Meanwhile people continue to get sick and die, argue and get divorced, lose their jobs and get depressed.

Elijah's Experience

For many years I have taken Elijah's story in 1 Kings 19 as a paradigm. Elijah has just pulled off a dramatic and successful confrontation with the prophets of Baal. But as soon as Jezebel finds out about it, Elijah takes off into the wilderness. He succumbs to fear and flight. His ministry is in shambles. He hides in a cave, reminding us of the depressed state of the discouraged minister. God tells him to go out onto the mountain. After the pyrotechnics of wind, earthquake and fire comes "a sound of sheer silence" (1 Kings 19:12). The unexplainable voice of God commands him to do the unthinkable: "Go, return" (1 Kings 19:15). Elijah experienced the crucifixion of ministry. Henceforth for Elijah ministry was possible only on the basis of the Word of God.

TWO SEASONS OF DYING

I suspect there are two major crucifixions or seasons of dying in ministry. The first happens early on, as studies now show. After seven years of higher education, great expectations of service in the Lord's vineyard often turn to sad and angry disappointment. About one third of those in early ministry leave, never to return. This is a major death, full of deep disenchantment and at times embittered recriminations. It is a personal, familial, fiscal and ecclesiastical disaster.

The second crucifixion is more subtle and less dramatic. It moves in on us more slowly and insidiously than the rapid, stunning disillusionment of the first crucifixion. It is more profound and in its way more deadly. Once endured and understood, it may usher in a resurrected theological conversion that makes ministry possible for the first time. It is the deep death and the real raising of our ministries. I suspect there are no surveys to consult here, and the timeframe is likely different in each case. There are no Kübler-Ross-like categories, but here is my impression of the typical order of events.

Once the first crucifixion is survived, the minister begins to realize the need for some serious skill learning beyond what the seminary offered. Further education may take the form of a doctor of ministry degree, which offers peer learning, theological retooling and skill enhancing. Some of us travel for a while in the rich pastures of spiritual renewal, all to our spiritual good. We begin to make our way along the career track. Workshops, conferences and seminars are grist to the surviving minister's professional mill. The pastoral tool bag gets filled up with all kinds of ministerial accoutrements, although sadly most ministers in North America are not reading very much these days.

Then somewhere along the way—ten, fifteen, twenty years out, who knows when or what circumstances precipitate the process—a terrible awareness begins to dawn. Now the hurt is deeper than before because it goes all the way down to the core of our being. It's not only a professional crisis; it is also a shattering crisis of faith. It is a theological crisis.

An inadequate theology leads to deep pain. *I can't do this.* I can't convert them. I can't heal them. I can't give them hope or make them happy or pray like Peter or preach like Paul. I can barely understand the theology books anymore, even when I carve out the time and energy to try to read them. My drawer full of pastoral, homiletical and administrative skills is impressive. The weight of experience is a great comfort to me, for I now know how to survive in a parish. But something inside tells me that the whole ministry enterprise is turning to sawdust. Inside I feel I can't bury any more babies, listen to any more divorcing couples, conduct marriages for any more pregnant girls, listen to any more tales of cancer diagnoses, conduct funerals for any more friends or preach the Beatitudes again. I have weathered too many arguments over the color of the church carpets, the brand of cookie for Bible school and bulletin covers for Mother's Day. The yoke is too heavy and the burden is too great to bear. Maybe I also discover that I am just plain bored.

Does God show up any more? If he doesn't, I can no longer carry the load, make the faith exciting or meet the demands for my attention. My knees are buckling under the weight of my obligations. My compassion recoils; it is killing me. And if God does show up, do I have the theological and spiritual apparatus to understand what is happening? If God does show up, what does that mean for what I am supposed to do and say?

A Test of Courage

It takes great courage for the seasoned minister to admit the second crucifixion. I suspect many of us don't. It may get buried beneath ecclesiastical bonhomie. Outward good cheer masks the inner death of compassion and the struggle for faithfulness. Keeping busy and running what my friend Eugene Peterson once called "the shop" may usefully occupy our days. We have learned how to fake it. A Doctor of Ministry class once insisted to me that about 90 percent of their time was taken up with congregational administration of one kind or another. I wondered, *What ever happened to the Word and sacraments?*

The darkness of Gethsemane is never welcomed. Its nights are too long and fretful, its prayers are too hard, its waiting is too lonely and its tears are too stained with metaphorical blood to be welcome. We stare into the spiritual void, into the theological abyss; we discover the terror of our personal *tohu wabohu* (the "formless void" of Genesis 1:2) and vaguely hope that the Spirit of God hovers over us as he did at the creation.

Not My Ministry

It takes great spiritual, theological and professional courage to look this second crucifixion in the eye and name it for what it is. This is the death of *my* ministry. From now on faithful ministry—God-glorifying, Spirit-empowered, world-transforming and kingdom-announcing ministry—will be possible only on some other basis.

The new basis is not something the seminary or the purveyors of ministry skills ever told us about. Our new basis for ministry is a sharing in the continuing ministry of Jesus, for the church and her ministry can be found only where Jesus has already showed up. He has to carry the load and do the job of saving people, for I am no longer capable or available. I have discovered a terrible limiting truth about myself. I am not the Messiah. I don't do salvation any more. I am being crucified; I am gone from the center of the picture.

The ministry of Jesus the Lord is displacing me from the throne of "my" ministry. In truth it was never mine. We refer to *our* ministries as if we own them and as if they are all about us. We deeply invest in our own success, although we wrap it up in pious language to soften its prideful aspect. We wish for professional preferment and fulfillment. We enjoy the applause and warm affirmations when they come. We are human, after all. We are made with boundaries we can't transcend.

When God Kills a Ministry

It is a mistake to leave the impression that our ministries are crucified only by the backbreaking burdens of responsibilities and obligations. Remember, the Word of God is combative; it is "sharper than any two-edged sword" (Hebrews 4:12). *Yahweh Sabaoth* is Lord of Hosts, commander of the heavenly army. God will not be timid about getting us out of the way.

Instead of *Where Christ is, there is the church,* we may have begun to think, *Where my ministry is, there is Christ and the church.* That idea is blasphemy, for we make ourselves Lord. In that case it is necessary for God himself to kill our ministry.

If we are not very successful in ministry, in whatever way we measure success, then God does not have a hard time getting us out of the way. It may even be a great relief when God brings us to the ministerial Jordan and says, *Cross and let me do it for you; stay here on this side, keep trying to do it yourself, and it's an early and resentful retirement.* The burdens of office may have become so heavy that we welcome being bumped aside by Jesus.

If, however, we aspire to ministerial royalty, then the crucifixion by God will have to be much more brutal. Some of us are upwardly mobile ministers. We have moved seamlessly from associate positions in prosperous congregations, under the guiding mentorship of able pastors, to solo pastorates and then to head-of-staff positions in large congregations where we can mentor others.

Those of us who are "successful" ministers should be warned that our mortification will be especially painful. We might be a long time dying. Our embedded pride and the myth of competence may lie very deep. Too easily we fell into the business of purveying religious merchandise to choosy consumers with measurable productivity and identifiable success.

NOT I BUT CHRIST

Whether we are "successful" or "unsuccessful" or somewhere in the middle, we get in the way. Whether we minister with mediocre skill or with truckloads of competence, whether with small success or with much public acclamation, God brings us to the point where our reliance on what we can do is killed by God.

The second crucifixion enables us to see the glorious freedom of ministry expressed by Paul: *Not I but Christ*. "It is no longer I who live, but it is Christ who lives in me" (Galatians 2:20). Everything is now to be rebuilt on this foundation. Jesus Christ stands in for us. As in faith and worship, so now also in ministry, he does for us what we cannot do for ourselves.

This is what I mean by the vicarious humanity and ministry of Jesus Christ. We are bumped aside by God with whatever forcefulness is required, so that Jesus stands in our place. He offers the worship, discipleship, faith and ministry that we thought we could offer but can't. The crucifixion of our ministry is staggering good news. Now ministry is now possible for us, probably for the first time, as gospel.

1

What's in a Name?

MENTALLY GLANCE AT YOUR CHURCH BULLETIN for this Sunday morning. Most likely it identifies you as the minister or pastor. It may also have a reference to the people of the church as the ministers. I do not recall ever reading in a church bulletin *Minister: Jesus Christ.* The necessary name is missing!

In whose name will we do ministry? It is the same question which the Jerusalem temple tribunal asked Peter and John. "By what power or by what name did you do this?" (Acts 4:7). On one level it is not a complicated question. Obviously we all do ministry in the name of Jesus and not in our own names. But how do we understand ministry in the name of Jesus?

We might answer that the Lord has authorized our ministry. For example, at the end of his parable of the Good Samaritan, Jesus said "Go and do likewise" (Luke 10:37). Left on this level, ministry looks like something we do in obedience to a command. Obedience has its proper place in the theological scheme of things. However, I am trying to build on a different foundation. I want us to build on what the Lord is doing before we rush to consider what it is we must do.

Minister: Jesus Christ

On a deeper level I am asking a more radical question that goes down to the roots of ministry. In whose name do we do ministry? What does it mean for the understanding and practice of ministry that the name of Jesus, as it was understood by the Christian community of the fourth chapter of Acts, indicates a present, acting and reigning Lord?

I am determined to ground our reflections about ministry in the person of Jesus Christ. Even before we reflect on the ministry of the Lord, we must grapple with his identity and his person. In every sense he and he alone is the authority for ministry and the actuality of ministry.

A Theology of the Name

The fourth chapter of Acts, with its theology of the name of Jesus, helps us come to terms with the priority of Jesus for the understanding and practice of ministry. Three name verses will guide our thinking: Acts 4:7, Acts 4:12 and Acts 4:30.

In this chapter I will reflect on the theology of the name of Jesus as it unfolds in Acts 4:7 and Acts 4:12, where we find established the singular authority of Jesus Christ. The rest of this book will be an extended reflection on Acts 4:30, where we read that ministry is performed through the name of Jesus. Such practical theology is truly radical, and I will try to unpack it as clearly as possible as we go along. While I will illustrate how the theology is lived out in ministry, this is a book about theology because it is a book about Jesus.

In the Name of Jesus

We will start with the basic story outline of Acts 3–4. Peter and John are going up to the temple for the midafternoon service of prayer. "A man lame from birth was being carried in" (Acts 3:2) to be placed at the entrance so he could ask for alms. Peter and John have no disposable income to help the man, but Peter offers him something he did not ask for. "I have no silver or gold, but what I have I give you; in the name of Jesus Christ of Nazareth, stand up and walk" (Acts 3:6). And he does!

Needless to say the healing greatly excites the crowd. Peter seizes the opportunity to preach. He interprets the Lord Jesus as the fulfillment of the faith of Israel and calls on the people to repent and believe that Jesus is Israel's Messiah (Acts 3:11-26).

Naturally the temple leadership is upset. They arrest Peter and John and the next day bring them before a hurriedly assembled tribunal of religious leaders. The scene is not hard to imagine. The religious authorities had thought that the Jesus movement had been dealt with by his execution. *We killed him; he's done with.* Now here are his apparent disciples healing people and saying that Jesus somehow is alive and doing deeds of power. They say he is *resurrected.*

The charge against Peter and John is the proclamation that "in Jesus there is the resurrection of the dead" (Acts 4:2). In the fervid theological and political atmosphere of occupied Jerusalem, upsetting the religious peace is a dangerous game. This spiritual insurrection must be put down once and for all.

WHICH GOD?

The public interrogation of Peter and John begins with the question "By what power or by what name did you do this?" (Acts 4:7). Notice the correlation between *power* and *name*. Perhaps it is not such an obvious correlation. They were asking "To what authority do you appeal? In whose name do you act? Which God do you represent?"

What is going on here is not a local squabble over fine points of theology. It is not the equivalent of a denominational debate or a theologians' roundtable. We have to appreciate that everything the old order stands for is assumed in the question "By what name?" The authorities' question expresses profound anxiety over the apparent emergence of a counterword which might displace the existing systems of authority, meaning, power and control. The leaders realize that everything is at stake: their job, their faith, their nation, their identity and their worldview.

If the name of this man Jesus is the name of power, if it means the actuality of God in present experience, then it is a fundamental challenge to the status quo. Everything apart from the name of Jesus is profoundly called into question, including every claim to power and authority, whether political or religious, social or personal, intellectual or moral.

We see the magnitude of what is at stake in the distinguished company who are assembled: Annas the high priest, Caiaphas, John, Alexander and all who were with the high priestly family, along with the rulers, elders and scribes. Everyone who has a stake in the old order has arrived for the questioning. Everything depends on the answer to "By what name?"

Gentle Jesus?

Perhaps we must stretch our imaginations to comprehend the radical quality of the threat posed by the resurrected Jesus to the political and religious authorities of the day. As North American Protestants we are quite comfortable with Jesus. How much do we allow him to threaten anything or anyone anymore? Certainly we have our moral issues where we challenge our culture's assumptions and behaviors in the name of Jesus. But I suspect for a broad swath of Christians, Jesus is a Lord at home in our celebrity-oriented culture: Jesus Christ, superstar. No tables get overturned. Rarely are demons denounced. No brood of vipers gets condemned. It is unlikely that authorities get provoked. Gentle Jesus, meek and mild. But that's not what is going on in the Scripture passage before us.

Same Question, Different Forms

The interrogators' question gets to the heart of things. "By what name?" The question ripples throughout the New Testament, though in different words, as the ultimate urgent question. Within it is embedded a total claim upon our lives with nothing excepted. John the Baptist sent two of his disciples to ask Jesus, "Are you the one who is to come?" (Luke 7:19). The fulfillment of the whole history and theology of Israel lay behind John the Baptist's question. Jesus asked his own disciples by the villages of Caesarea Philippi, "Who do people say that I am?" (Mark 8:27). In John's version Peter responds, "We have come to believe and know that you are the Holy One of God" (John 6:69). Paraphrasing this: "Your name is Yahweh, Yahweh saves." It is either the most appalling blasphemy or the *logos* of truth alongside whom there is no other truth.

Jesus is Lord. Are we anymore capable of being stunned by that claim? Frankly I am not sure that we are. The unfamiliar has become all too familiar. What if this Jesus is not at home in our church, our culture or our worldview? Then we might understand something of the threat which the name of Jesus poses to all other claims to ultimate authority.

Who Are You, Lord?

"Who are you, Lord?" It is the question of Saul on the road to Damascus when he is confronted by the light and the voice from heaven (Acts 9:5). The question will provoke our reflections well beyond this chapter. Not only faith itself but the whole of ministry turns on the answer.

For Saul the question totally devastates him and changes his life and his ministry forever. Like Elijah before him, Saul is commissioned for ministry by the Word of God. The question he asked concerns the identity of truth, meaning and reality in no disguise. Saul asked it with a willingness to deal head-on with the answer. I will address the question "Who are you, Lord?" under the Acts 4:12 declaration of "no other name." In the next chapter I will reflect on the appropriate priority of asking the "Who?" question in Christology.

For now let us stay a little longer with the question "By what name?" because it opens up aspects of the deep confusion within both church and society concerning truth, authority, meaning and value. *By what name* will I live and act? *By what name* can I accurately interpret history? *By what name* is there a ground for hope beyond the ravages of divorce, cancer, abuse, war and death?

Between Two Extremes

We walk a fine line here because we must pick our way between at least two competing worldviews. The clash between them and the success of either will form the potentially tragic history of the twenty-first century.

On the one hand we see around us a culture, both popular and intellectual, tipping headlong into postmodernist relativism. It insists, *Leave me alone with my truth*. That is the genesis of the diversity gospel we hear everywhere today. At its deadliest it ends in nihilism. Consider the body-pierced, tattooed images of the rock and sports stars who are thrust in front of our children on mainstream media. Who can doubt that we are rushing headlong into the moral abyss?

On the other hand, we also see around us a world grasping at absolutes and even killing for them. We see it in the amazing and deadly appeal of various religious and political fundamentalisms.

We ride the pendulum as it swings between two extremes. On one side is metaphysical chaos with its culture of self-destructive hedonism and dumbed-down ethics, summed up in the ubiquitous catchword *Whatever*. On the other side is metaphysical rigidity with violent, sometimes deadly consequences for disobedience.

The impasse between the two extremes locks churches and society in its grasp. Indeed the contemporary world with its intensifying internecine warfare is in part the result of this partisan bifurcation of experience. As the philosophical structures of the modern world collapse, is the only choice between chaos and absolutism? Is there another option? Is there another way?

Who Is Truth?

"By what name?" The question does not pose the issue of truth in any abstract manner. It does not lend itself to either ideological deconstruction or exclusive doctrinal affirmation. The question of truth is now posed as a personal question.

Suppose that the central issue of truth is not the nihilistic claim that there is no truth or the liberal query "Which truth?" or the absolutist claim of this truth and no other. Suppose those are all false options and the real question is *Who is truth?* What if truth at its heart is about a relationship with a person before subscription to an idea?

If priority is given to the "Who?" question, it is appropriate and even necessary to ask, *What then is the truth's name?* We should not merely ask, "In what do I believe?" Instead we should ask, "In whom do I believe?" Truth is about being in love rather than being right. Truth is lived in terms of a relationship with God and not in terms of vindication.

Christians understand that we are not right, for no one is righteous. Only God is right. Because Christians understand truth specifically in terms of the *name*—that is, the *person*—of Jesus, truth is about a person and a relationship with that person which he has established from his side.

Communion with God

Christianity at its core is not about subscription to a theological system or the authority of a sacred text or ethical perspectives, although they are all important. Christianity at its core is about the self-referenced claim by a person who said, "I am the way, and the truth, and the life" (John 14:6). That person calls us into relationship with himself, which means communion with God. He showed and taught us that his way is love and mercy and forgiveness. His truth is not just his teaching but his person. His life is life indeed because in union with him we have communion with God.

The Christian claim is that at the end of the day, at the end of life, you and I have to deal with Jesus. Christianity is about a person and therefore it is about personhood. That means a great deal when we deal with other people, especially people who differ from us in their faiths, ethics, political ideas and worldviews.

Jesus Waits at the Beginning

Recently I heard a lecture by an English Methodist who is both a scientist and a Christian theologian. He was talking about the scientific debate over the Big Bang, and he used an image that I found quite arresting. He told us that physicists have pushed backwards in time to 10^{-47} of a second after the Big Bang. I am not a physicist; I am not sure what that figure means other than that it is an infinitesimally small period of time. As physicists push back to the beginning of everything, the models of the laws of physics seem to unravel. Our mathematics can't cope. Then he said something like this: I imagine some brilliant theoretical physicist sometime soon pushing back to the beginning of all things. It will be like climbing a huge incredibly difficult mountain. And as the physicist struggles over the final intellectual ledge to see the beginning of creation in all its staggering immensity and intensity, that physicist will see Jesus sitting there waiting with a smile of greeting and welcome.

If Jesus is the eternal *logos* come in the flesh of his humanity, as we believe he is, then such a scenario is quite plausible. Ultimate truth is a person who has a name, whether in physics or in theology.

Not What or How, but Who?

Pontius Pilate asked the wrong question when he confronted Jesus and asked "What is truth?" (John 18:38) The question of truth is a not a *What?* or a *How?* question but a *Who*? question. Ultimately physics and every other sphere of human inquiry will end up having to give the answer *Truth's name is Jesus.*

Now I will go where wise angels fear to tread and take the risk of saying something quite provocative. One of our evangelical sins arises because we forget that our savior is a Person rather than an idea or a list of propositions or a moral code or a creed. We commit the sin of *essential tenetism.*

Essential tenetism is a form of idolatry. It arises out of giving priority to the *What?* question rather than the *Who?* question. *What* do you believe? Well, I don't believe in what I say, the form of words I use or my manner of expression. I don't believe that the central mystery of faith is reducible to words, as if I can capture the living Lord Jesus with my theological concepts. To claim such would be the height of theological arrogance. I don't confess "I believe in the Nicene Creed and all it stands for." Rather in confessing the Nicene Creed I am directed away from the words to the One in whom I believe, Jesus Christ, Lord of all.

In heaven there will be no theologians as theologians and no creeds because there will be no need for theology. There will be only brothers and sisters of the Lord Jesus, all of whom will see the Lord face to face. Theology, creeds and denominational traditions will all pass away.

I believe in the One to whom my words point, just as I believe in the One to whom Scripture points, namely the Lord Jesus Christ. Of course some words point to him more accurately and faithfully than others. It is right to fuss with that. I do that for a living as a professional theologian. But don't confuse the words with the real thing, the person of the Lord.

Independently of Jesus Christ, whose name alone we plead, there is no other or prior authority. All metaphysical notions like authority and tradition are under his rule. All things are under his feet, under his judgment and under his grace. At the name of Jesus every knee will bow.

AN UNEXPECTED NAME

A few years ago when I was renewing my British passport, I dug out my birth certificate to make a copy for the application process. On the front of the certificate in beautiful calligraphy is my name, Andrew Purves. All my life I had been told I had no middle name. I was told that since I was born six weeks prematurely, there was no time to decide on a middle name. My parents had not even agreed on a first name for me. I was not expected to live. My Irish Catholic mother sent down to St. Mary's Cathedral in Edinburgh, and on the second day of my life a priest came to the hospital to baptize me.

As I pondered my birth certificate, I turned it over and found in the top right corner the cramped notation in Latin of my baptism. To my utter amazement I discovered I had a middle name! I ran downstairs and announced to my three teenage children that I had a middle name.

"What's your middle name, Daddy?"

"Well, it's my father's mother's maiden name."

"What's your middle name, Daddy?"

"Well, it's the name of a minor nineteenth-century Scottish novelist."

"Daddy, we don't care. What's your middle name?"

"In fact, it's quite a common name in the border region of Scotland."

Voices were now raised. "We don't care! What's your middle name?"

I replied, "Hogg."

At that point my children took great delight in snorting out, "Daddy's a pig!"

A Person's Deepest Identity

Names mean identity. People are formed by their names. The question *What's your name?* is an inquiry into a person's soul. It ventures into the person's deepest identity and personhood. To know someone's name is to know him or her. To call a person by name is to be in relationship with that person. That's why it is such a violation when the car salesperson or insurance salesperson calls me by my first name on first meeting. It is a violation of my personhood for the sake of a sale. It is manipulated intimacy. I protect my own name as I must honor other people's names.

Saul asked "Who are you, Lord?" (Acts 9:5). He meant "What is your name?" Peter told the assembled Jewish authorities "There is no other name under heaven given among mortals by which we must be saved" (Acts 4:12).

So what's in this name of *Jesus?* The Savior has many titles besides the main ones *the Christ* and *the Lord.* I have counted thirty-nine names for him in Scripture. Some are rather curious, such as the Bright Morning Star (Revelation 22:16), the Forerunner (Hebrews 6:20) and the Guarantee (Hebrews 7:22). Others are more familiar: the Lamb (Revelation 5:6), the Word (John 1:1) and the High Priest (Hebrews 8:1). But he had only one name, *Jesus,* and his name designates the only One in whom there is salvation. It is the name that is above every name, the name before which everyone and everything shall bend the knee and acknowledge him for who he is.

An Earthly Name

In the Gospels our Lord is called *Jesus* almost six hundred times. The expression *Jesus Christ* occurs only four times. *Lord Jesus* occurs only twice and both are disputed texts (Mark 16:19 and Luke 24:3). Please refer to William Barclay, *Jesus As They Saw Him* (SCM Press, 1962) for some of what follows.

When the Gospel writers thought about the Lord, they did not use lofty theological terms. They simply called him by his name, Jesus. He was not an abstract idea or a moral principle. He was not the subject of a theological oration or creed. He was a man with a given name, flesh and bones, born of a woman called Mary, born within the religion of the Jewish law during the time of the Second Temple and military occupancy by the Romans.

The sheer use of his name Jesus carries the significance of his earthliness as opposed to otherworldliness. In later centuries the church would struggle to hang on to his blunt actual humanity. But in the Gospels it is not a problem. His name connects him to earth and to actual carnal flesh, in*carn*ation.

Jesus was a common name at the time of his birth. It is still common in Spanish-speaking cultures. It is the Greek form of three Hebrew names: Joshua, Jehoshua and Jeshua. In his history of the Jews, Josephus mentions about twenty men called Jesus, ten of whom were our Lord's contemporaries. Yet by the second century the use of the name had all but vanished. It disappeared among the Jews because it was hated, and it disappeared among the Christians because it had become singularly holy.

The Significance of Names

My name tells you about me. My name Andrew was my paternal grandfather's name. My baptismal middle name Hogg roots me in my paternal grandmother's family. It has the effect of locating me. It says I belong. It identifies me as somebody.

In the biblical world names also carried significance. Now and then they also carried a message. As an extreme example, think of the names of Hosea's children. Jezreel means "the Lord will punish"; Lo-ruhamah means "the Lord will not have pity"; Lo-ammi means "not the Lord's people."

Jesus was given his name by the direct intervention of God. An angel of the Lord appeared to Joseph, telling him to take Mary for his wife, for her child was conceived by the Holy Spirit. "She will bear a son, and you are to name him Jesus, for he will save his people from their sins" (Matthew 1:21). The rabbis had a saying: "Six persons received their names before they were born, namely, Isaac, our great lawgiver Moses, Solomon, Josiah, Ishmael, and the Messiah" (Barclay, p. 11). God himself would name his Messiah. The name would tell us who he is. It would be a one-word summary of everything he stood for. His person and his work would be gathered up in one word, his name. He would be called Jesus.

God Names Himself

God names himself, a point some people have a hard time getting their minds around. God's name is not something we dream up to satisfy our theological fancies or ideological proclivities. "God has sent the Spirit of his Son into our hearts, crying, 'Abba! Father!'" (Galatians 4:6). The theme that God names God is perfectly consistent in Scripture from the I Am of the burning bush to the name of the Savior to the name Father.

In Hebrew the name Joshua means "the Lord is my help" or "my rescue." As the angel said to Joseph, "he will save his people from their sins." The name tells us who he is; he is the Savior.

In Greek the name is *Iēsous*. The Greek theologians connected the name with the verb "to heal," *iasthai*. There is no real connection except vaguely in sound. Nevertheless it allowed the point to be made that there is healing in the name of Jesus, for he is *ho iomenos*, the Healer and the Good Physician. Peter, filled with the Holy Spirit, declared before the examining tribunal that the lame man had been healed "by the name of Jesus Christ of Nazareth" (Acts 4:10). The notion that Jesus is the healer has obvious New Testament grounds. So the Greeks regarded Jesus as the great healer of both souls and bodies. With this point we draw closer to the center of his ministry. We too are often bold to say, "In the name of Jesus, you are forgiven; in the name of Jesus, be healed."

Charles Wesley exalted the healing name of Jesus in his hymn "O For a Thousand Tongues to Sing."

> Jesus! the name that charms our fears,
> That bids our sorrows cease,
> 'Tis music in the sinner's ears,
> 'Tis life, and health, and peace.

The Anointed One

The name of Jesus carries the hope of history. It also carries hope for each one of us. Thus he has the supreme title "the Christ," which is the Greek translation of the Hebrew word that means "the Anointed One." It is a title rather than a proper name. Jesus Christ means "Jesus the Christ" or "Messiah Jesus." The title fleshes out everything that is contained in his name, linking it all specifically with the history and expectations of Israel, now universalized to include every nation and people within the scope of his ministry.

Now it is but a small step to the big claim. If Jesus is the Lord's anointed, if he is God's salvation present here in the flesh of his humanity, not as a representative of God like the prophets of Israel, not as an earthly agent of mediation like the Old Testament priests, not like the kings who led God's people on God's behalf, not as an intermediary being who is not quite God and oddly human as the heretic Arius taught, not only as a brilliant religious and moral teacher, then . . . With overwhelmed senses and inadequate theological categories we can only stutter aloud along with Paul, "Who are you, Lord?"

We are staggered at the immensity of the claim as we first mutter the words with our hands clasped over our mouths. Yet the words must also be shouted from the mountaintops and spoken to every person on the face of the earth. We proclaim that Jesus is the Lord. Jesus is Yahweh Sabaoth. Jesus is God!

No Longer Shocking?

Jesus is God. We hear it so often that it becomes old stuff. We are no longer shocked by it. How do we make the familiar unfamiliar again, as Karl Barth once asked, so that we might drop to our knees overcome with spiritual gratitude for who it is that we meet here? "And the Word became flesh and lived among us, and we have seen his glory, the glory as of a father's only son, full of grace and truth" (John 1:14).

It took the church over three centuries to begin to get her mind around some of what all this means for the understanding of God. Great creeds and long complex theological treatises were eventually written. The debates were enduring, often violent and frequently deadly. Perhaps the conclusion is well summed up in a statement of St. Athanasius of Alexandria in the 360s. Writing of the meaning of Jesus, he said that not only was God *in* Christ, not only did God work *through* Christ, but that God came *as* the man Jesus. *God as the man Jesus.* That is the staggering immensity of what we are considering. That is the mighty claim which defines the heart of Christian faith. That is the sole content and non-negotiable center of Christian doctrine and ministry.

Dealing with God

When we deal with Jesus as he is attested for us in Scripture and proclaimed in the worship and teaching of the church, we are dealing with God. Jesus is not someone who tells us about his insights into God. He is not a wonder worker for God. He is not a moral genius. He is not the greatest religious teacher who ever lived. He is not a wandering eastern sage of great wisdom.

Jesus is worshiped because he was and is God. He is the creator Word, the saving Lord, the reign-of-God-establishing *pantokrator,* Lord of all. There is no secret God hiding behind the back of Jesus, furtive and unknown, whom we must periodically reimagine to suit our changing ideology. Jesus, in the flesh of his Mary-given humanity, is God. God is none other than who he is for us and for our salvation in, through and as the man Jesus. Through him, in union with him, which is the principal work of the Holy Spirit, we know the Father, serve the Father and worship the Father in spirit and in truth. That is what "no other name" means.

> He is the image of the invisible God, the firstborn of all creation, for in him all things in heaven and on earth were created, things visible and invisible, whether thrones or dominions or rulers or powers—all things have been created through him and for him. He himself is before all things, and in him all things hold together. He is the head of the body, the church; he is the beginning, the firstborn from the dead, so that he might come to have first place in everything. For in him all the fullness of God was pleased to dwell, and through him God was pleased to reconcile to himself all things, whether on earth or in heaven, by making peace through the blood of his cross. (Colossians 1:15-20)

> Let the same mind be in you that was in Christ Jesus,
>   who, though he was in the form of God,
>   did not regard equality with God
>   as something to be exploited,
> but emptied himself,
>   taking the form of a slave,
>   being born in human likeness.
> And being found in human form,

he humbled himself
and became obedient to the point of death—
even death on a cross.
Therefore God also highly exalted him
and gave him the name
that is above every name,
so that at the name of Jesus
every knee should bend,
in heaven and on earth and under the earth,
and every tongue should confess
that Jesus Christ is Lord,
to the glory of God the Father. (Philippians 2:5-11)

He's the Whole Deal!

Let us be bold to draw some provocative conclusions from our key verse, Acts 4:12: "There is salvation in no one else, for there is no other name under heaven given among mortals by which we must be saved."

First, we sometimes hear the rumblings of the silly question "What's the big deal about Jesus?" It was a question that recently rocked my own denomination, the Presbyterian Church (USA). The answer, of course, is that Jesus is not a big deal; he's the whole deal! He's not a name on a list; he's the whole list. That is what it means that he is Lord. The whole list is under his grace and judgment. Everything else in faith, life and ministry has truth only in relationship to him. All other questions and issues pale into insignificance beside the New Testament's cosmic and historical claim concerning Jesus.

Christians are defined by being grounded in and committed to this one name, the name of Jesus as Lord. We understand everything else in faith and life in terms of that name. If we lose ground concerning the single, saving lordship of Jesus Christ and his significance, the church will truly be apostate.

Preach Christ

The second conclusion I draw is that the only mission strategy which will encourage our congregations, usefully employ our clergy, enable history-changing and kingdom-of-God-anticipating ministry, and enable us to evangelize with any degree of faithfulness and power is the preaching that there is salvation in no other name. To ministers let me say this as strongly as I can. Preach Christ, preach Christ, preach Christ. Get out of your offices and get into your studies. Quit playing office manager and program director, quit staffing committees, and even right now recommit yourselves to what you were ordained to do, namely the ministry of Word and sacraments. Pick up good theology books again: hard books, classical texts, great theologians. Claim the energy and time to study for days and days at a time. Disappear for long hours because you are reading Athanasius on the person of Jesus Christ or Wesley on sanctification or Augustine on the Trinity or Calvin on the Christian life or Andrew Murray on the priesthood of Christ. Then you will have something to say that's worth hearing.

Remember that exegesis is for preaching and teaching; it has no other use. So get out those tough commentaries and struggle in depth with the texts. Let most of what you do be dominated by the demands of the sermon as if your whole life and reason for being is to preach Christ, because it is. Claim a new authority for the pulpit, the Word of God, Jesus Christ, over you and your people. Commit yourself again to ever more deeply becoming a careful preacher of Christ. Don't preach to grow your congregation; preach to bear witness to what the Lord is doing, and let him grow your church. Dwell in him, abide in him, come to know him ever more deeply and convertedly. Tell the people what he has to say to them, what he is doing among them and within them, and what it is he wants them to share in. He is up to something in your neighborhood, if you have the eyes to see and the ears to hear. Develop a christological hermeneutic for all you do and say. Why? Because there is no other name, that's why.

Spend Time with Jesus

The third conclusion I draw is that we must spend time with Jesus. If he is as important as I am suggesting he is, as the faith tells us he is, as you know he is, then he is worth our time. In fact he demands our time.

To repeat the result of a recent survey by Michael Jinkins of Austin Theological Seminary: 62 percent of the Presbyterian ministers interviewed had no or little spiritual life. That is alarming to me. Henri Nouwen, the late Dutch Roman Catholic priest, once wrote that you cannot minister in the name if you are not living in the name. Take John 15:1-11 to heart. Abide in the Lord, for apart from him you can do nothing. I take Jesus' statement to be not hyperbole but a matter of fact. The Lord will transform you and your congregation. The real thing is Christ. Abide in Christ.

Rejoice Always

Finally, because there is no other name and because we live in that name, "Rejoice in the Lord always; again I will say, Rejoice" (Philippians 4:4). The creed got this right: the chief end of man is to give glory to God and to enjoy him for ever. The angel said to the shepherds, "I am bringing you good news of great joy" (Luke 2:10). Jesus said, "I have said these things to you so that my joy may be in you, and that your joy may be complete" (John 15:11). We have been named by the Name; we have been claimed by the Name; the Name will not forget our names.

Whatever the evil one hurls at us, rejoice. Whatever the travails of ministry, rejoice. Be of good cheer; the Lord has the victory because we are held unto all eternity by the one who has the Name, who is the

Name, the Name that is above every name. Again I say rejoice, for there is no other name under heaven given among mortals by which we must be saved.

Now what does it mean that ministry is *through* the name of Jesus? The rest of the book is an extended answer to that question.

2

Who Are You, Lord, and What Are You Up To?

Ministry Is Who God Is and What God Does

I HEARD A SERMON IN THE SEMINARY CHAPEL, delivered by a nationally known guest preacher in excellent homiletical style, in which we were urged to be more purposefully active in prophetic discipleship. Examples of the church militant were paraded before us, and we were instructed to go and do likewise.

I sat in my pew and sagged, weighed down by the guilt lashing, depressed by all the *oughts, shoulds, musts* and *have tos*. It does not matter what theological label we put on that preacher, for we hear the same message from liberal and conservative preachers. The message is that we are responsible for bringing in the reign of God. It is our burden to actualize what God creates only as a possibility, or even worse, what God gives as an invitation to a task we must fulfill.

Guilted into Discipleship

We hear the appeal to muscular activist Christianity so often we might begin to think it is the real thing. We get guilted into discipleship. One of the most difficult aspects of Christian life and ministry is how to understand the gospel through and through as *gospel* and not turn it into law, into obligation and into demand.

Consider Paul's words in Philippians 3:12: "Not that I have already obtained this or have already reached the goal [of having been made perfect]; but I press on to make it my own, because Christ Jesus has made me his own." The capacity to press on is the result of being seized hold of *(katalambano)* by Christ. The verb is intensive, even aggressive.

If being a Christian means that faithfulness is up to me to press on, run the race and strain forward to bring in the kingdom of God, and if all the focus is on my response and my obedience, then I am doomed. Why? Because much of the time my response is too woebegone, too feeble, too uncertain, even too unfaithful to be adequate or worthy of God.

What is the gospel for lower energy Christians? What am I supposed to feel or do when I discover that I can't raise the dead, heal the sick, mend the marriage or undiagnose the cancer? Christian faithfulness is possible only because Jesus Christ has us grasped firmly by the scruff of our spiritual necks and will not lose hold.

No Substitute for Jesus

In the introduction we pondered how harrowing and humbling it is to realize that our ministries are not redemptive in any serious rendering of that term. The test case for ministry is that Jesus present by his Spirit shows up and does something only God can do.

Only the ministry of Jesus is redemptive. No amount of religiously motivated helpfulness or niceness can fill in for the redemptive ministry of Jesus Christ. The danger for us and especially for our parishioners comes when we insist on displacing the ministry of Jesus with our own ministries. When that happens our ministries must be crucified.

Books and classes on the ministry of the church must have Jesus Christ and his ministry at their core. But they must have him at their core in a very specific sense, namely to teach who he is and what it means that he had a ministry yesterday, that in the power of the Spirit he has a ministry today, and that he will have a ministry tomorrow when he comes again.

In this chapter I want to explore these issues in particular: Who is Jesus, and what sense do we make of his present ministry that he actually does here and now?

With this chapter we make the turn to the task of practical theology and to the unpacking of the conclusion to the believers' prayer at Acts 4:30: "Signs and wonders are performed through the name of your holy servant Jesus." Now we begin a journey of theological conversation concerning the ministry of the present and acting Lord. We will look at what it means that our thinking about ministry begins with reflection on God's ministry as we know it in, through and as Jesus Christ, wherein God encounters us as a present, acting and reigning Lord, not now in the flesh but in the power of the Holy Spirit. He said, "Remember, I am with you always" (Matthew 28:20). The plain meaning is that Jesus promised to be present. What I want and need to know is this: *Who are you, Lord, and what are you up to?*

A Desperate Prayer, a Quiet Answer

I remember lying in hospital after cancer surgery, wondering what the upcoming six months of chemotherapy would be like and whether I was going to make it through the process. *What I need now,* I thought, *is not a theological treatise to edify my mind, though that has its place, not some sense that God in Christ is in solidarity with me in my suffering and fear, though that too is helpful. What I need is a God of power. I need a God who acts to change things.*

As I cried out, “Save me, Lord!” I did not expect any rending of the heavens. What I did hear in an inner way was the quiet word of the God who acts. It was a voice heard by a lonely, fearful, pain-filled, morphine-dominated fifty-six-year-old man. God said to me that whether I lived or died, I did so unto the Lord, and he would not abandon me.

Not everyone gets healed, and that is a great mystery, but the promise of his peace is not an empty promise, and it is given for all who know him. God acts. I believe it even when God acts in ways that utterly confounds my expectations.

ALWAYS IN THE PRESENT TENSE

God acts. We believe it. Specifically we claim that in the Spirit, Jesus acts. What does it mean that he acts? How does he act? What does his acting mean for how I should act? Practical theology is theology concerned with action. It is the *So what?* in the power of the Name. It is an attempt to enter into the deep mystery of what it means that we do and say all things through Jesus Christ our Lord.

All things are done through the name of Jesus. His person and work are always in the present tense. God acts through the person of Jesus, who as the ascended Lord ever lives as the continuing mediator between the Father and us and between us and the Father, in the freedom of his love and in the power of the Spirit. Through himself, whose name is Jesus, who is the Christ, he brings us to the Father of our spirits.

Miss what it means that everything is done and said, believed and hoped for, through the name of Jesus, and everything in the gospel is suddenly turned on its head to become law, duty, obligation and responsibility. Miss the *through* ministry of Jesus and we are well on our way to being Christians who look as though we have spent forever sucking on a pickle—joyless, exhausted and embittered!

"WWJD?"

Professor Ray Anderson of Fuller Theological Seminary once made the observation that the WWJD question was the wrong question. For several years many of our young people have worn bracelets on their wrists with the initials WWJD. The purpose is to remind the wearer to ask in every circumstance, "What would Jesus do?" Accordingly, Christian action is based on following the moral influence and teaching of Jesus.

Following Anderson's insight, my main problem with the theology of WWJD is that it turns Jesus into the teacher of fixed moral ideas which must be imitated. Everything is now cast back upon us to achieve. Even with a little help from the Holy Spirit, it sounds like a religion of obedience to moral laws.

Today's prevailing paradigm for pastoral work and ministry flows from a basis similar to WWJD. We can call it the *lingering aftereffect* theory of ministry. Jesus is perceived to enjoin caring for one another in times of difficulty, following what the late Princeton Theological Seminary professor Seward Hiltner, father of the modern pastoral care movement, called the Good Samaritan principle: Get yourself where wounded people lie hurt and help them. The motivation for action is the continuing moral influence of Jesus, and our job is to acquire the skills necessary for competent action. In other words, the pain sets the agenda; ministerial skill in action is the solution. To put it more formally, pastoral care in this theological framing has an anthropological starting point. We understand ministry as primarily something *we* do.

It is right to have a high regard for ministry skills. Caring is morally good. Ministry without appropriate skills leads to malpractice. But if all that goes on in ministry is religiously motivated caring, no matter how skillfully done, it is thin fare indeed. Our ministries are not redemptive in any meaningful sense of the word. It is not faithful to the gospel to regard our ministries as the agency of the redemptive presence of God. Something much more radical is yet to be discovered.

WHO DOES THE MINISTRY?

Is ministry something we do, or is ministry something Jesus does? The answer, of course, is *Yes*. We have a ministry, but it is derivative. It depends in every way upon the continuing ministry of Jesus. His ministry is in the present tense. This is the good news. He is not Lord in name only, but also in act, and not only in past act, but in present and future act.

Ministry is a theological act. What makes ministry theological is what makes it ministry: *God acts*. God acts today as God has always acted, in, through and as his Living Word, Jesus Christ. God acts through the continuing ministry of Jesus, who is present to and for us in and by the grace of the Holy Spirit.

To say God acts means first that God does not act behind the back of Jesus, as if Jesus were now redundant or incidental to the wider purposes of God. The New Testament affirmation of the single lordship of Jesus Christ is still, and always will be, in place. God's ministry for salvation has an irreducible christological character.

To say God acts means second that Christian faith, life and ministry are not built upon an idealized and mythic meaning system, but upon a personal relationship with a Lord who acts today in time and space in his continuing ministry of grace, love and communion. We are familiar with the language of a personal relationship with the Lord Jesus. But it may be a new idea to think about a personal relationship in terms of sharing or participating in his ministry. The magnitude of this is overwhelming in its actuality as good news for the work we do.

To say God acts means third that the emphasis is always placed on Jesus Christ and not on us. The focus is on Christ's promised faithfulness to be present to and for us as God who loves, forgives and blesses us. The focus is not on our experiences of being loved, forgiven or blessed, important as these are. Most important, but often omitted from consideration, Christ's promised faithfulness to be present for and to us is as the human One who offers to the Father the life and ministry that is acceptable to God.

All this is for the glory of God and for the sake of the world. The issue for pastoral theology is not our reflection on *our* experiences of God, valid as these are in their own place, but on *the God whom we experience* in, through and as Jesus Christ in the power of the Holy Spirit.

Christ Makes Ministry Possible

I invite you to risk the thought that God shows up as more than the posthumous influence of Jesus or as the vague hovering of the Spirit. Something much more radical than the call to skillful caring is at work. Of course we should not exclude asking, "What would Jesus do?" There is an appropriate place for the moral influence of Jesus. But it is more important to ask, "Who is Jesus Christ for us today and what is Jesus doing here and now, in this hospital room, during this committee meeting, in this service of worship, in this counseling session and so on?"

To participate in Christ's ministry means that I share in his life. Sharing in his life means that who he is and what he is up to defines the whole work of my ministry. Wherever Christ is and wherever we are joined to him, there truly is the intentional, disciplined and faithful ministry of the church. It is not our ministries that make Christ present; it is the present, living Christ who makes our ministries possible.

We will take this whole book to discuss the two momentous concerns for the practice of Christian life and ministry: (1) to determine specifically and actually who Jesus Christ is for us today, and (2) to consider what it means to say that we are joined to the life and ministry of this present, acting and reigning Lord.

I recall with fondness and gratitude the Dogmatics 2 class in New College, Edinburgh, in the early 1970s. James B. Torrance, with characteristic enthusiasm and clarity, would insist on the priority of the *Who?* question over the *How?* question for our reflections on Christology. Everything in theology depends on knowing who Jesus Christ is and what it means that he is confessed as Lord and Savior. If we go astray at the beginning by asking the wrong question, we will never grasp the radical heart and significance of the gospel. Christianity's central doctrine—Jesus Christ is Lord!—is given as the answer to the question: Who is the incarnate Savior of the world?

Setting out the priority of the *Who?* question places us on the trajectory of thought that characterizes the classical theology of the church. James Torrance was instructed on this point by Dietrich Bonhoeffer. In the early part of his book *Christ the Center,* Bonhoeffer opens up in a remarkably insightful way the core methodological issues we deal with in Christology and therefore in ministry. Bonhoeffer's starting point is the required beginning for what today we would call a nonfoundationalist Christology. Enlightenment philosophers do not set the boundaries for our Christian reflections on the identity of Jesus Christ. They do not tell us what is allowable to believe and what is not. When we are encountered by the living Christ, the only valid question is Saul's Damascus Road question: "Who are you, Lord?" It is this question which Christology must answer and which sets the enquiry on its own proper ground.

We do not begin Christology or our thinking about ministry with a question about the capacity of history to receive transcendence. Rather, we begin with the fact that it did, and we go on from there. When we ask "Who are you, Lord?" of the incarnate Savior of the world, the answer cannot be given in terms of reflection on human experience, but only on the ground the Lord Jesus gives himself. We do not fit Jesus into our prior categories of thought; rather, our knowing of him must be transformed by who he is in his own right as we are encountered by him.

THEOLOGY WITH FEET ON THE GROUND

As always in theology and in our understanding of ministry, actuality is prior to and constrains that which subsequently becomes possible in knowing and doing. Theology that has its feet on the ground, rather than floating speculatively in the air, is theology that is obedient to the sheer self-giving of Jesus Christ, who confronts us actually and really.

It is only after Jesus Christ has revealed himself and confronted us and by his Spirit drawn us into a relationship with himself that we ask aright, "Who are you, Lord?" The enquiry is conducted on his terms by which he has established us, not on our terms by which we might hope to establish him. There is no ground for knowing Jesus outside of Jesus himself and what it means that by his Spirit he has brought us into union with himself. There can be no independent reason for Jesus Christ that has authority to ratify him as the truth and actuality of God. He is self-attesting just as he is self-revealing. It is only through God and on God's terms that God can be known.

ENLIGHTENMENT WATERLOO

With Jesus Christ, autonomous human reason has reached its limits. The Enlightenment experiment, which tried to impose universal human reason on theology, has met its Waterloo. Apart from who he is in his own identity and being, and as he gives himself to be known by us, Christology and ministry have no possibility. The *Who?* question we put to Christ is concerned to discover more fully the identity and meaning of the risen and ascended Lord who has already addressed us and claimed us as his own.

We pursue our christological enquiries on the basis of the fact of

Christ and not according to a previously determined metaphysical or epistemological necessity established independently of Jesus Christ. In a more technical idiom, we can say that theology is conducted according to *a posteriori* and not according to *a priori* thinking.

To sum up this difficult material somewhat whimsically, if the creator of the cosmos wants to walk on water, he can walk on water! The theological response is not "How did you do that?" but "Who are you, Lord?"

Jesus meets us as Savior and Lord, as Emmanuel who is both God with us and God for us. Allow me to play with some words to make my point. He does *Who he is*. Because he does *Who he is,* we are not *What we do,* but in union with Christ we are *Who we do*. Jesus' *I am* leads to his *I do,* as it leads subsequently to our *I do*. Knowing him, knowing thereby his ministry and through union with him sharing in his life, is the center of all practical theology.

A Pastoral Call Example

The ministerial imperative is the consequence of the christological indicative. The christological dog wags the ministerial tail. Let us consider a specific example of how it works out in practice.

It is Thursday afternoon, 2:00 p.m. Imagine yourself as a minister about to make a pastoral call on Mrs. Smith, a homebound member of your congregation. Theologically, what is your agenda? As you press the doorbell, what—or better, who—will determine how you spend the next hour?

Because ministry is a theological act, God in, through and as Jesus Christ, in the freedom of his love and the presence of his Spirit, is actively and redemptively encountering Mrs. Smith. Can you identify what it is the Lord is up to? Assuming you recognize him and identify the Lord's present ministry, what are you supposed to do?

Let us not run too quickly to attend to your responsibilities just yet.

Let us stay with the primary theological issue that the pastoral visit must try to address. Who is Jesus Christ for Mrs. Smith today? Let us say, for example, that it is a month after she has buried her husband.

A well-informed pastoral christological awareness of who Jesus is, and thereby what Jesus is doing here as Lord for Mrs. Smith on this Thursday afternoon at 2:00 p.m., with all of the contextual specificity regarding him and her that you can discern, guides all that you will say and do. After all, it is *his* ministry, not yours, that will heal and bless, save and comfort Mrs. Smith. It is his ministry that is primary, for his ministry alone is redemptive for Mrs. Smith. To suggest anything less is to render Jesus as an absent mythic Lord or as a moral idea you have to incarnate, neither of which is much help for Mrs. Smith. Beware of all teachings that suggest it is your job to incarnate Jesus or to stimulate some kind of ostensible religious experience. The Father already sent the Holy Spirit to Mary. It is not necessary for you to try to repeat the incarnation within yourself in an attempt to be messianic!

I hope it is already evident that you do not bring Jesus with you on your visit. He is already there with Mrs. Smith, present and acting in the power of the Spirit. It is his actuality that gives you a ministry. It is his Spirit-mediated presence and act that makes your ministry possible, not the other way around.

This does not mean Jesus Christ is a vague spiritual process that somehow works its way out in the pastoral call, an implicit Christ immanent within the pastoral event yet hidden, unannounced, and at best perhaps only obliquely acknowledged. Neither is the efficacy of Christ's ministry reducible to felt experiences. What is not felt is taken on faith as we cast ourselves upon the promises of God. We trust God to be faithful to what is promised in the gospel. Your job is to identify and bear witness to who Jesus Christ, clothed with his gospel, is for Mrs. Smith today and to allow your pastoral visit to proceed on that basis. Of course, you have to believe that Jesus Christ is a present, acting and reigning Lord!

The ministry of Jesus Christ here and now in Mrs. Smith's living room is the basis for and the content of your ministry. To put it more formally: the actuality of the ministry of Jesus Christ is the ground for the possibility of your ministry. Apart from sharing in this actuality, sharing in Christ's present life now through union with Christ, you have no ministry. Remember that Jesus said, "Apart from me you can do nothing" (John 15:5). Our ministries wither for lack of being engrafted onto the vine, in which case it is no bad thing when they are gathered up and thrown on the fire and burned.

Two Models of Ministry

Let me lay two models of ministry side by side. They are in sharp contrast to one another. I have to ask your trust that the first model is not a straw man but based on an actual event accurately reported. Let it be said that this first model of ministry has a secular context, while the second has a congregational context.

A student told me that during the first days of a summer unit of Clinical Pastoral Education he was given a model for professional ministry. Everybody, he was told, has something that oppresses them. Your job as a hospital chaplain is to assist people to bring the feelings from that oppression to the surface and then to draw from within themselves the strength to overcome it. You connect with people on the ground of their own agenda and needs. Ministry means drawing out the latent possibilities for healing that lie buried within. It is not your job to introduce God language or to provide a theological commentary on the person's situation.

The second model, the one I am proposing, insists that the primary skill for ministry is a deeply formed pastoral christological awareness arising directly out of our theological and spiritual formation. In other words, our life in Christ with head and heart is what we need to be about. We know our parishioner Mrs. Smith. We know Jesus Christ. Most important of all, we know that Jesus Christ is a present ministering Lord to whose life and ministry we are joined through union with Christ. It is as this threefold knowing comes together in us, the ministers, that by the grace of God what we do becomes a pastoral theological act. We bear witness to the God who acts as Jesus Christ, now in the presence of his Spirit.

Christological Timidity

Too often we have too small an understanding of Jesus Christ and of what it is that he is up to. A tragic feature of much recent pastoral theology and thus pastoral care is its christological timidity. We forget that an encounter with the living Lord to whose presence we bear witness is the heart of Christian faith and ministry. We must attain some measure of disciplined theological acuity as we address the question *Who is the incarnate Savior of the world and what is he doing—here, today, now, in the specific ministerial context that engages me?* The soul of ministry is the God who encounters us in, through and as Jesus. The acting presence of Jesus in the agency of his Spirit is the ground of all ministry.

Who is the incarnate Savior of the world? It is not a theoretical question. Being encountered by him is not a neutral datum of experience. Saul, encountered by the risen Lord on the Damascus Road, did not ask a speculative "Who?" question (Acts 9:5). He was shaken to the core of his being as he was questioned by the voice that spoke out of the flashing light. When we ask with Saul "Who are you, Lord?" we are trying more faithfully to understand who this God is who has revealed himself to us, encountered us and brought us into relationship with himself precisely in, through and as the man Jesus of Nazareth. It is a question put by faith, not by unfaith. It is a question put in Christ, not apart from Christ.

FOUR CENTRAL EVENTS

In order to explore the depths of the question *Who is the incarnate Savior of the world?* we may reflect on the four great event mysteries that are central to Christian faith: the incarnation (which includes the atonement), the resurrection, the ascension and Pentecost. We open up a sight path that throws light upon the subject of Jesus Christ when we think about Christmas and the life of Jesus up to and including Good Friday, Easter morning, Ascension Day and Pentecost. The church and Christian faith stand or fall on the reality and truth of these events.

The incarnation. Let us reflect briefly on the incarnation, the *becoming carnal* of God. The incarnation is the downward movement of God by which God as one particular man enters history by becoming part of God's own creation but without ceasing to be God. It is the event in which faith associates the eternal God with a contingent fact of history and attributes a saving significance to it. It is summed up in one staggering sentence from John's Gospel: "The Word became flesh" (John 1:14). God saves in a human way precisely as this man Jesus. Here is the truly amazing claim of Christian faith. We must not back away one bit from its particularity and universality.

This man Jesus Christ in his flesh is God the Son of God who is Savior and Lord. Had the Word not become incarnate, Jesus would not have existed. The One who is the incarnate Savior of the world is truly a human being. He is bone of our bone, flesh of our flesh, born of a woman, born under the law. St. Athanasius in the 360s put it this way: the consequence of God becoming flesh is God *as* Jesus.

We must stress the significance of the incarnate life of Jesus Christ for the atonement and our salvation. Jesus Christ is in himself our salvation, not only in what he does for us, but also who Christ is for us in the unity of his divine and human personhood. It is not incarnation by itself that accomplishes our redemption. As the incarnate Word,

Jesus Christ acts *personally* rather than instrumentally on our behalf. The atonement takes place within his incarnate life, thereby falling both within the life of God and within human life.

The relation between the Father and the Son is not contained within or limited to external, moral or juridical relations, as we find often in highly rationalized penal theories of the atonement. It is rightly expanded to include a profoundly personal and ontological relation, so that it is God who saves as the man Jesus. This salvation penetrates to the depths of the human condition. The atonement is not an external work of God upon us which leaves our humanity untouched, but an act of God personally from within the depth of our humanity and on our behalf. By it we are not only forgiven but transformed into persons who now, through Jesus Christ and in the power of the Spirit, are in communion with the Father. We are healed, we can say, from the outside in and from the inside out.

None of this is to circumnavigate the meaning of the cross. Calvary remains the event in which the terrible consequences of our human rejection of God are borne out to the fullest extent. I am trying to say that (1) the atonement is worked out within the person of Jesus, and (2) the life and death of Christ have to be very closely held together in our minds in a personal way and not apart from who Jesus is.

The resurrection. It is necessary to understand the personal identity of Jesus in the light of the resurrection. The basic essential message is that Jesus who was dead is now alive, raised in his humanity by the power of God the Father. The consequence of humankind's sin-separation from God is borne by Jesus and thereby borne away. Here we are confronted with the insurmountable mystery of the correlation of God's holiness and God's love. We should not collapse our soteriology into either pole, but live and believe within the mystery that presents itself. He is risen! The crucifixion has not ended Jesus' ministry. The resurrection means that in Christ there is a future for *our* humanity, for what happened to Jesus is what will happen to those who are in Christ. When we ask "Who are you, Lord?" we have to say in response "He has been raised" (Mark 16:6).

This raised human Jesus is not a ghost. He was raised in his body. There is now a future for creation, including for physical bodies. God has not abandoned our flesh, which would imply that it is rather nasty stuff and not as precious as our souls. We are saved in the embodied fullness of our humanity.

The ascension. We come now to the often forgotten doctrine, the ascension. This is the upward movement of Jesus by which the now alive human Lord returns to eternity to continue his ministry. The neglect of Jesus' ascension in liturgical and pastoral thinking and practice is fatal to our ministry.

The ministry of Jesus does not end with his resurrection. In his ascension he does not abandon his humanity. He is not the ascended Lord apart from everything that has happened between his incarnation and resurrection. Borrowing an insight from Gerrit Dawson of First Presbyterian Church, Baton Rouge, Louisiana, we can say that by his ascension the past incarnate ministry of the Jesus who was raised from the dead becomes through his Spirit present to every age and person. The earthly ministry of Jesus that was past and particular now becomes present and universal.

Without the ascension Jesus' ministry remains in the past, even given his resurrection. It is not enough for us to believe that he who died for us is alive again. He must yet reign in power and be present in ministry. By his ascension he ever lives *to continue the ministry he had while on earth*. In this sense the disciples are no more privileged than we are. The Lord who was there with them is, in his Spirit and freedom, here with us. It should be clear why I said that the loss of the ascension is fatal to our ministries. If Jesus is not now a present, acting and reigning Lord, it is completely up to us to do something messianic in imitation of him; and that is beyond our abilities, although we flail around and tragically keep trying.

Jesus' ascended ministry is not something new or different in content from the ministry he exercised while on earth. As in the flesh he was spiritually present to those to whom he ministered, now ascended he is spiritually present to us through the Holy Spirit. He is the same Lord, the same spiritual presence (thought not now in the flesh of his body) and he does the same ministry, which has at its core our restoration to communion with the Father. What is his ministry?

First, he ever lives to present us to the Father, so that in Christ and through Christ we are holy and blameless in love before God (Ephesians 1:4).

Second, he continually prays for us.

Third, he sends us the Holy Spirit to be the form of his presence with us.

Fourth, the sending of the Holy Spirit completes the God-enacted drama of salvation and creates the ground of the church's ministry.

Pentecost. God the Father through God the Son sends us the Holy Spirit for two principal reasons. First, it is the Lord's chosen way of being present. Second, it is in order to join us to this present, acting and reigning Jesus Christ and to share thereby in who he is and in what he does, thus enabling the church's ministry. This theological point is summed up in the doctrine of our union with Christ. It is the dynamic basis for all ministry in the church.

Christ's Present Ministry

Let me bring this part of the discussion to a close by paying homage to perhaps the most influential book I have used in nearly a quarter century of seminary teaching: *Worship, Community, and the Triune God of Grace* by James B. Torrance (InterVarsity Press, 1997). Torrance is the late Scottish theologian to whom I referred earlier when introducing the priority of the *Who?* question. While the book is specifically about the recovery of a Trinitarian understanding of worship, the central point applies across the board. By our union with Christ, we share in Christ's present ministry. What is this ministry?

According to Torrance, through our union with Christ we share in his communion with the Father and in his mission from the Father to bring others into that communion. Christian life is characterized by the dual consequences of our life in Christ: worship and ministry. This is the meaning of being a Christian. This is the core practical theology of Christian faith.

Who, then, is the incarnate Savior of the world? He is the present, acting and reigning Lord. His name is Jesus; his title is Messiah, Christ. He is the Christmas, Good Friday, Easter, Ascension and Pentecost Lord.

MINISTRY DEPENDS ON JESUS

I have placed a large burden on the present ministry of Jesus Christ. In fact I am trying to allow Jesus to bear the whole load of ministry, every ounce of it. I see no hope for our ministries otherwise.

Every meaningful question concerning the significance of Jesus for Christian faith is posed in the present tense. *Who are you, Lord, and what are you up to?* Any other perspective turns him into an antiquarian curiosity who can't quite be fitted into present experience. Our access to the ministry of Jesus Christ today is through knowledge of his past ministry as it is attested for us in Scripture. Because he is "the same yesterday and today and forever" (Hebrews 13:8), an understanding of who he was and what he did in the flesh of his incarnation is the divinely given way of knowing the nature and content of his present ministry.

Our knowledge of Jesus and his ministry, even of his present ministry, is not a mystically intuited knowledge. Rather, it is knowledge of Jesus, come in the flesh.

The Ministry of the Triune God

Our focus is upon the ministry of the Triune God of grace as God gives us to know him in, through and as the person and ministry of Jesus, son of Mary. It is summed up in the apostolic benediction "The grace of the Lord Jesus Christ, the love of God, and the communion of the Holy Spirit be with all of you" (2 Corinthians 13:13).

The grace of the Lord Jesus Christ. Words like *grace, love* and *God* are a minefield of trouble because we think we know what they mean. Dietrich Bonhoeffer taught that grace apart from Jesus Christ is no grace at all, for grace is Jesus Christ and Jesus Christ is grace. Grace apart from Jesus Christ, Bonhoeffer famously taught, was cheap grace, grace as an idea or a principle rather than a person. Apart from its specific anchoring in the actuality of the gospel, grace becomes unhinged from the reality that gives it meaning and truth. Jesus Christ is the actuality of God, for "in him the whole fullness of deity dwells bodily" (Colossians 2:9).

The grace of the Lord Jesus Christ is the grace of God, from the Father, through the Son and in the Holy Spirit. It is not something apart from the whole act and being of the Trinity. Grace implies both the whole of God and the full message of the gospel. The grace of the Lord Jesus Christ is the mission of God to save in, as and through the man Jesus.

Grace means Jesus; grace is Jesus. He is Emmanuel, for he is God with us. More than that, his name tells us who he is. *Yeshua* means Yahweh-Savior, the One who "will save his people from their sins" (Matthew 1:21). The incarnation directly implies the atonement, and there is no atonement without the incarnation. Otherwise God has not come among us and dealt with us precisely in, through and as this man. Thus Jesus is worshiped as *Iēsous Kyrios*, *Lord Jesus*. Grace has no Christian meaning apart from this confession.

Coming as Emmanuel who is Savior, Jesus lived the singular human life as it was intended by God in filial obedience and love toward

God and toward those to whom he came, although "his own people did not accept him" (John 1:11). His life was lived "full of grace and truth" (John 1:14). The manner and nature of his life led to his death. While it was on one level an ordinary though violent human death, on another level, because of *who* he was and because of what occurred on the third day, his death was redemptive, as God's act to forgive and to save. Looking through the lens of the resurrection, his life and death were seen to be God's act and therefore of saving significance. Because Jesus is Lord it was seen then that God had really come to earth, becoming flesh, entering into the ghastly plight of our human life unto death under the holy judgment of God.

Because Jesus took on flesh and because the range of his atonement includes all things, we and the creation of which we are a part now have a future that is entirely God's doing. The atonement has a past and a future reference, a retrospective and a prospective dimension. Jesus Christ comes not just as one who forgives but also as one who restores us to a new relationship with the Father. It is not yet the atonement that our sins are forgiven; we must still be restored to communion with God and to a new and otherwise unavailable *at-one-ment*. The grace of God does a new thing. It opens the kingdom of God, that is, communion with God, to all who are in union with Christ.

Grace, in summary form, is (a) tied specifically to Jesus Christ and (b) is God's operation by which we are saved, that is, forgiven and restored to communion with God. *Grace* is inherently a theological word that characterizes God's reconciling, forgiving and communion-restoring love toward us. Paul testifies to "the good news of God's grace" (Acts 20:24). It is good news or gospel because it is entirely unearned, being God's sovereign and unconditioned choice to act freely and objectively in, through and as Jesus Christ and through the Holy Spirit. Grace is God's saving action in history. It is "God's purpose of election" (Romans 9:11) being fulfilled in, through and as Jesus of Nazareth.

Grace does not leave us passive. In grace *(charis)* the Holy Spirit, who is the "Spirit of grace" (Hebrews 10:29), gives to each Christian his or her particular grace-gift (*charis*ma), which is to be expressed in thankfulness (eu*charis*tia) in Christian service and ministry. The more literal translation of Hebrews 12:28 reads, "Let us have grace" *(charin)* rather than "let us give thanks, by which we offer to God an acceptable worship with reverence and awe." In his commentary on Hebrews, John Calvin introduced an indicative rendering of this verse congruent with the main idea, taking it to mean that we have been given the grace that enables us to worship and serve God faithfully. Empowered by grace-giftedness, the Christian life is thankful response to God. The proximate goal of the gospel is lives of fruitful and joyful discipleship in the power of the good news.

This understanding of the grace of the Lord Jesus Christ has two defining implications for pastoral work. First, pastoral work must give the highest priority to the kerygmatic affirmation "You are forgiven." The whole movement of the gospel pulls in this direction. Second, pastoral work must help people identify grace in their lives in its specificity as forgiveness of sins and equip them to be faithful in the thankful response of Christian discipleship through their communion with God.

Too often pastoral work has been interpreted as responding to needs, hurts and all kinds of personal problems. Left out from the ministry has been the concern to call people to lives of fruitful and joyful discipleship in the power of the good news. Their homecoming to God is of such reality and power that it is lived out in joy. Pastoral work must not only respond to the negative but act as the midwife of the positive, for we have received "grace upon grace" (John 1:16). No matter what the sin, grace abounds all the more (Romans 5:20), meaning that all things pertaining to the Christian life are based on grace.

The love of God. The familiar words "God so loved the world" (John 3:16) characterize the ministry of God, revealing the divine nature and purpose. The ministry of God arises out of the very being of God, for "God is love" (1 John 4:16).

God's love for us is not an occasional divine virtue. Love is not an attribute of God. Love is who God is within the divine intra-trinitarian relations and in his relations with us. God's act within history in, through and as Jesus Christ expresses the being of God who loves eternally within the communion of the Father, the Son and the Holy Spirit, one being, three Persons. The New Testament builds upon the conviction that there is an unbroken and eternal relationship in the Spirit between Jesus Christ and the Father. Over and against any thought that the church or human faith should occupy center stage in the understanding of the Christian faith, the New Testament posits the centrality of the Father-Son relationship. Everything in Christian faith and life arises out of this relationship, sealed in the unity of the Holy Spirit.

The Father-Son relationship is described as the *agape* with which the Father loved the Son even "before the foundation of the world" (John 17:24). Jesus Christ is revealed as God's Son, showing that God's Fatherhood and Christ's Sonship belong to God's eternal being. The relationship between God the Father and God the Son is inseparable. The Son alone exegetes the Father, for the Son is "close to the Father's heart" and "has made him known" (John 1:18). He is loved by the Father (John 5:20) and knows the Father as the Father knows the Son (John 10:15). Indeed the Father and the Son are one (John 10:30) so that whoever has seen Jesus Christ has seen the Father (John 14:9).

The love that flows between the Father and the Son in the unity of the Holy Spirit reveals that God is a God of love within the communion of the holy Trinity. God is both loving and being loved. God's love is the basis for Christian confidence in God; for who God is toward us in, through and as Jesus Christ, God is always in himself. Nothing "will be able to separate us from the love of God in Christ Jesus our Lord" (Romans 8:39).

Jesus' ministry is the incarnation of the love of God. Interestingly, the synoptic Gospels have only one reference to the love of God (Luke 11:42). Yet the Gospel accounts are replete with the mercy and compassion of God in Jesus Christ. Consider Jesus' healing of the sick, his companionship with those cast out from society and synagogue, his sense of oneness with the poor and his life laid down for sinners. He lived what he taught. He loved them and therefore God loved them with a power and authority that brought them into God's company.

There is not some hidden, secret God lurking behind the façade of God's love in Jesus Christ, ready to judge us capriciously rather than in love. Even when we stand under the judgment of God, it is through the love that God has for us in Jesus Christ, who died for us and rose in power to bring many sons and daughters to glory. Who is to condemn us when Christ is our judge? The love with which the Father loves the Son is the love which Christians share through their union with Christ. This love is not possible within the natural capacities of human experience and will. It is entirely the result of abiding in Christ the true vine (John 15:1-11). It is an alien love, not our own but entirely the fruit of being in relationship with Jesus Christ.

The Christian life and its possibility are appropriately summed up in the conjunction of the indicative and the imperative in John 15:9: "As the Father has loved me, so I have loved you; abide in my love." The ministry of the love of God means that through union with Christ we stand not only under grace, but in the love that flows eternally within and among and from the Father, the Son and the Holy Spirit. Through grace we are saved by and for the love of God.

Abiding in God's love is directly related to obeying Christ's commandment to love one another in a way similar to the love Christ has for us (John 15:12). Love is far greater than an emotion; it is an act of will and obedience. The only ground for its possibility is as the fruit of our union with Christ. We can be commanded to be lovers because we have been chosen and appointed by Jesus Christ to be fruitbearers (John 15:16), because we share his fruitfulness.

The communion of the Holy Spirit. The grace of the Lord Jesus Christ and the love of God lead irresistibly to the reality and empowerment of the communion of the Holy Spirit, in whom all that has been said thus far concerning the ministry of God becomes ours for and in the living of the Christian life.

The Holy Spirit is the personal presence of God by whom God brings us into communion with himself through relationship with Jesus Christ. The work of the Holy Spirit is a Christ-related event. It is a God-glorifying, person-empowering and church/mission-creating event. Because the Holy Spirit binds us to Jesus Christ, we are bound by the same Spirit (to use James Torrance's formulation) to share in Christ's communion with and mission from the Father. The Spirit calls the church into existence to be a community of worship and ministry through her union with Christ.

Our communion is with the Father through our Spirit-led union with Christ. Consequently it is also communion with one another as we are formed into the ministering Body of Christ, the church. For this reason we do not speak of communion *in* the Holy Spirit. We speak of the communion *of* the Holy Spirit, meaning communion *with and in Christ.*

When the Christian tradition teaches the communion of the Holy Spirit, it means union through the Holy Spirit with Jesus Christ himself. Union with Christ is not the imitation of Christ in which we try to follow the example of Jesus. Instead, more radically, the Christian life is participation in Christ's righteousness, holiness and mission through the bond of the Holy Spirit. Our being and becoming Christian is not something that we work out through our heightened religiosity, morality, activity or spirituality. It is first of all a divine initiative.

As in being forgiven, so it is also in our being and becoming saints. God in Christ through the Holy Spirit provides for us. Christ is our sanctification (1 Corinthians 1:30). We are conjoined to Christ by the unilateral work of God through the Holy Spirit in what Calvin called a "mystical union" (*Institutes* 3.11.10). By the bond of the Holy Spirit we become one with him and share in his life. Calvin's term "mystical union" parallels Paul's term "in Christ," meaning that God through the Holy Spirit saves us by engrafting us into Christ.

As the consequence of our union with Christ through the Holy Spirit, we share in his communion with the Father. That which is his by nature as Son becomes ours through grace by adoption. Here is the center of Christian worship and prayer, whereby through our union with Christ we share in the filial life of love between the Father and the Son in the unity of the Holy Spirit. It is summed up in the words "we declare to you what we have seen and heard so that you also may have fellowship with us; and truly our fellowship is with the Father and with his Son Jesus Christ" (1 John 1:3).

The center of Christian faith and life is our sharing in the love or communion within the holy Trinity and in the ministry that flows from it. This also means that we have communion with one another. We cannot have Christ as our Savior and God as our Father without having the church as our community of faith. The communion of the Holy Spirit means the communion of the Body of Christ and sharing in Christ's mission from the Father for the sake of the world. Belonging to Christ's fellowship means sharing in his ministry.

"Rooted and grounded in love" and growing up "in every way into him who is the head, into Christ" (Ephesians 3.17; 4:15), we share in

Christ's ministry from the Father. Since piety and action are intimately related, Christian discipleship is understood both intensively and extensively as communion with God and as service of God in the life of the world. United with Christ through the bond of the Holy Spirit, the church is driven by the two imperatives: to worship and to serve. We serve the people first by serving God in union with Christ. The congregation may pay our wages, but God gets first claim on us.

In union with Christ, the church of the Easter and Ascension Day gospel is also and necessarily the church with a gospel mission. In union with Christ, the church is given a mission from beyond herself. It is not the world in its own analysis of its needs that sets the agenda for the church, but Jesus Christ in his being sent and sending. In the power of the Spirit and in union with himself, he sends the church out, as a parallel with his own sending by the Father in incarnation and atonement.

3

The Crucifixion of Ministry

Christ in Our Place

WE DO NOT MEDIATE JESUS CHRIST. We do not make him effective, relevant or practical. Neither is it up to us to raise the dead, heal the sick or forgive the sinners. Faithful ministry is just not that grandiose.

When we think that the ministry of the gospel is for us to do, that we carry Jesus around with us in our pastoral and homiletical tool bags, dispensing him here and there as we deem fit, we are in the way and have become a hindrance to the ministry of the gospel. As ministers of the gospel we are not ecclesiastical conjurors with magic hands, pulling Jesus out of our hats.

To repeat, here is the issue: *Our ministries are not redemptive.* Only Christ's ministry is redemptive. If we stand in the way, focusing on our ministries, we have to be shoved out of the way. When we have a severe preoccupation with "my ministry," that ministry has to be crucified.

Show and Tell

In class I often use a show-and-tell example to illustrate the central point for the understanding of ministry. I invite a student to join me at the front of the class. I always pick a large, strongly built man. Let's call him Bob. I have Bob stand in front of the class, perhaps in a posture of prayer with his hands raised and his face tilted upward. I provide a commentary that goes something like this: God has called Bob to be his man in ministry. Bob is a pious man who heeds God's call, goes to seminary, travels successfully through the ordination process, is ordained and is sent off to be minister in Timbuktu Church. After he survives the initial bumps in the road, a number of realities begin to dawn on Bob. He finds it hard to be faithful in prayer and Bible study. It is some time since he read a decent book on theology. He is always busy and always tired. Rarely does he expend himself at tasks he thought ministry would involve. Administrative and programmatic obligations overwhelm his time. Pastoral responsibilities get pushed aside. Conflicts with colleagues and parishioners demand his energies. He wearies at the kind of preparation he knows he is supposed to put into his sermons. In short, Bob has found that ministry is not much fun anymore. He feels the burden and weariness of his call and almost nothing of the anticipated joy and fulfillment.

A Mighty Push

I then move alongside Bob and give him a mighty push which sends him stumbling across the room. The push is the displacement that I call the crucifixion of ministry. Then I, representing Jesus, stand in for him. I stand in his place and I have Jesus say, "I, not you, do the ministry that saves and heals, that gives hope and blesses, that forgives and promises new life." This is the kinetic paraphrase of Galatians 2:20, "I yet not I but Christ." Speaking for Jesus, I say to Bob that I am sending the Holy Spirit to join him to me and my ministry. I tell Bob to come behind me, put his hands on my shoulders and rest against me, for I will do the ministry in his place. The primary work of ministry is not up to him anymore. Indeed, it never was. Hitched to Jesus, Bob is bidden to enjoy the ride.

Bob has to come to terms with his displacement. It is his crucifixion. The good news, but also the difficult news for any of us to hear, is that our ministries are not redemptive. Only Christ's ministry is redemptive, and by the Holy Spirit we are joined to it. This means for us a process of ministerial *metanoia*—getting a new mind regarding ministry. It involves a reorientation of the theology and practice of ministry according to sharing in the continuing ministry of Jesus.

The goal of this chapter is to lay the theological foundation for understanding that in all things we rely on Jesus Christ, who offers to the Father in our place the life of faith, worship and obedience that God desires, and who in the Spirit joins us to himself to share in his self-offering.

Two Forgotten Doctrines

In my dramatic action with Bob I have illustrated two hugely important doctrines that come out of the ecumenical theological consensus of the historic church. They have been more or less forgotten amid pragmatic responses to the pressures of ministry today. The doctrines are *the vicarious humanity and ministry of Christ,* and *our union with Christ.* Together those two doctrines give us the basic framework for the understanding and practice of ministry. They are the sum of practical theology.

In this chapter we will think especially about the ministry of Jesus Christ in which, in our place, he responds to the Father in filial obedience and love. The following chapter will discuss what it means that we are joined to his ministry.

Seized Hold Of

I was preaching at a large summer gathering of several congregations. My text for the sermon was Philippians 3:12: "I press on to make it my own, because Christ Jesus has made me his own." My theme was that because we have been grabbed by the scruffs of our spiritual necks by Jesus Christ, there is a chance that we can run the race, press on and strain forward to what lies ahead. In my sermon I placed the emphasis on Christ having laid hold of us. As noted earlier, the Greek word is *katalambano*, an intensive word meaning "to seize hold of."

The crowd was so large and dense that not many people could greet me afterward. But one fellow determinedly sought me out and angrily demanded to know why I had downplayed the place of human decision. "You can't be saved without a response, *your* response. You've got to make a decision for Jesus!" he insisted loudly, poking a finger at my chest.

Struggling for calm, I answered, "Yes, there is a need for a response to the Word of God. But the good news is that Jesus makes that response for you. His response is the first response, just as God's Word is always the first Word. He stands in for you, doing for you what you are unable to do or won't do for yourself. That's our spiritual condition as a result of the Fall. Your responsibility is not to try to say *Amen* in your own strength, as if everything depends on that. When we think we have done so, all too often it leads to pride. Your responsibility is to say *Amen* to Christ's *Amen* that he says first of all for us, and in the Spirit now says in us. I liken it to Galatians 4:6. 'And because you are children, God has sent the Spirit of his Son into our hearts, crying "Abba! Father!"' What you rely on is not your response, but his on your behalf."

Needless to say I did not convince my questioner. As he turned away from me I suspect he was muttering unkind words about the heresies taught in seminaries today by theologians who don't get it. It was one of those interchanges that lead me to sit in my car for a few quiet minutes to calm down before driving off, wondering what all that was about.

Not in Our Own Strength

I am not convinced that my interrogator really believed in a present, living and reigning Lord who acts on his behalf, bringing him to the Father in his, that is Jesus', name. He really did not believe that his capacity to respond to God was in need of redemption. He thought he could respond to God in his own strength. His was a reductionist Christology masquerading under cover of evangelical piety. Our response of faith, repentance and obedience is the Spirit-led consequence of Christ having seized hold of us, not the condition for it.

To get some perspective on what is at stake here, let us turn to one of the most important theologians of the church, Athanasius of Alexandria (A.D. 296-373). He lived through, and made perhaps the most important contributions to, the great theological debates that raged through the early and middle decades of the fourth century. He was a decisive contributor to the writing of the Nicene Creed in A.D. 325 and played a huge role in the subsequent defense of orthodoxy in the ensuing theological battles against the Arian view that Christ was less than God. In the 360s he wrote his important treatise *Four Discourses Against the Arians*, a long and complex work that is one of the greatest theological contributions to the church's thinking about Jesus Christ. (It is published at www.newadvent.org/fathers/2816.htm.)

First let me set the scene. As theological students at the University of Edinburgh in Scotland in the early 1970s, my wife and I remember well the lectures we heard on Nicene Christology. They were given by the brothers Thomas and James Torrance, two formidable scholars of doctrine who would swoop into the lecture hall, academic robes flying, as a collective hush fell on the room. Though I cannot quote their exact words, here is the gist of what they tried to teach us.

> You come to the study of theology, and indeed you stand before God Almighty, with many questions. *What* is the meaning of

Jesus' life? *How* could he have been raised from the dead? *Why* did Christ have to die? *When* will he come again? But these are not the questions you should be asking! The prior and primary question for Christian faith is not *What?* or *How?* or *Why?* or *When?* but *Who? Who* is Jesus Christ? That is the question you must answer. That is the question that the Council of Nicaea addressed.

A War for the Mind of the Church

The bishops gathered in A.D. 325 ready to wage a war for the mind of the church because there was disagreement about the answer to the fundamental question, Who is Jesus Christ? Dissension had existed in the church as to the person and nature of Christ almost from the beginning, but in the fourth century two champions arose and rallied others to their theological standards. They were Arius and Athanasius.

The rallying cry of Arius was the oft-repeated slogan "There was when He was not." The *He* is Christ. Arius and his followers meant that Christ was created by God and was therefore in some way different from God, who is eternal. In the concern to preserve the primacy and unique holiness of God the Father, the Son's status and essential being were subtly diminished. He was seen as less than God.

Athanasius and his supporters countered the claims of Arius with a term borrowed from Greek philosophy, *homoousios,* which means "of one or the same being or essence." They argued that the Son and the Father share the same stuff. That is to say, Jesus is fully God.

The Years After Nicaea

The years following Nicaea were marked by political intrigue, theological ambushes, banishments and a disquieting ebb and flow of doctrine about Christ. Athanasius himself was exiled from Alexandria five times in the continuing theological tug-of-war over the true nature of Christ.

In A.D. 431 at the Council of Ephesus, the Nicene Creed was reaffirmed and the use of any other creed was banned. Twenty years later the Council of Chalcedon gave final ratification to the orthodox position. The boundaries had been finally and firmly set, and the central mystery of the faith was protected.

That is the brief history. We are concerned now with the specific presentation of the ministry of Jesus Christ embedded in the heart of Athanasius's position.

Athanasius's Argument

Here in a nutshell is Athanasius's argument: *Jesus Christ ministers the things of God to us and the things of humankind to God.* That statement, virtually a direct quote from Book 4 of the treatise, is well worth taking time to ponder.

There are three points to consider as Athanasius develops what this means. (1) God saves through and as the man Jesus; that is, Jesus of Nazareth ministers the things of God to us as God. (2) As such, as a man Jesus receives the Word of God on our behalf. (3) Jesus ministers the things of humankind to God, again on our behalf.

First Athanasius emphasizes that Christianity must speak of a real incarnation of God in the flesh of the man Jesus. "The Word became flesh" (John 1:14). That is not a metaphor. Jesus was not man who then became God. Rather God, the Son of the Father, became a man without ceasing to be God, and this for our salvation. The incarnation is a real irruption of God into history. When we deal with Jesus we are not dealing with a representative of God, but with God. Who God is in Jesus Christ is who God is.

To emphasize the point, Athanasius suggests that Christ was not promoted from a lower state, but was God who took the form of a servant. Thus, says Athanasius, we must speak so: not God *in* a man, but God *as* the man Jesus.

REAL, NOT APPARENT

In the incarnation, Jesus' humanity is not a means to an end. It is not something external to his being or in addition to the gospel. Athanasius's point is that God does not work through the man Jesus as though the humanity of Jesus was merely the vehicle of grace and in the end disposable. Rather, the incarnation means that God comes to us and for us *as* the man Jesus in a particularly personal way. God saves as this man. His becoming flesh is real not apparent. God came among us as the son of Mary in the personal particularity of his actual history.

What is intended by Athanasius when he states that Jesus Christ is the Word of God to humankind, or that he ministers the things of God to us? Although Athanasius uses the Nicene word *homoousios* only once in his treatise (at 1.9), the meaning of the Nicene affirmation runs through the argument in no uncertain manner, for everywhere he builds on the central truth that Jesus is one in essence or being *(homoousios)* with the Father. He is the very image of the Father, an icon of the Father, so to speak. He is the Word, Wisdom and Radiance of God.

Thus Athanasius understood that God is antecedently and eternally in himself what he is toward us in the Son. We see the Father in the Son, and we contemplate the Son in the Father. Athanasius shows that through Jesus Christ, God has definitively accessed our world. God has entered into the dire plight of humankind to bring forgiveness of sin and restoration to communion with the Father. These insights are critical both for knowledge of God and for confidence in salvation through Jesus Christ.

According to Athanasius, as Jesus Christ God has really come among us, indwelling our history in his flesh as the actual Word of God in such a way that he is the place where God speaks and acts in saving love toward us and for our salvation. Jesus Christ is God for us. Though the Father gives it, the Son is the gift, says Athanasius. The incarnation falls within both the sphere or reality of God and the sphere or reality of humankind. Jesus Christ is the sole mediator between God and humankind, bringing God to us and, as we now turn to consider, us to God.

Vicarious Humanity

Second, we must notice Athanasius's argument that Jesus Christ not only is God's Word to and for us, but also as a man, he hears and receives God's Word on our behalf. With this point, and more fully in the next, we turn to what has become known as the vicarious humanity of Christ, a doctrine that is critical for my argument.

This point that Jesus is both God's Word spoken in our flesh and received and heard as a man is a truly radical theological insight. It moves Athanasius toward his goal to show that salvation is 100 percent God's work. What is at stake here? Athanasius regarded us as not having a free mind but as a people under sentence of death. Furthermore, we could not become sons and daughters of God other than by receiving the Spirit of the true Son.

The argument presupposes that even were God to speak, outside of the Spirit of the Son hearing on our behalf, we would not hear and receive that Word, for only the Son can hear the Word of the Father. So Christ is not only the One who spoke forth the Word of God, but also the One who received the Word of God when he took flesh, not for his own sake, but for our sakes.

To make clear what this means, Athanasius insists that in so receiving, Christ as the Word of God received nothing that he did not possess before. It is in the flesh, as the man for us, that the one who is the Word of God received that Word in his humanity for us. Jesus Christ then is both speaking God and a hearing man, and this for us.

Third, we now consider the saving work of Christ in his human agency, in which he ministers the things of humankind to God as the high priest of our confession. This aspect of Christology is quite neglected by many theologians, with catastrophic consequences. What, or rather *who* Christ offers is himself, and his offering of himself to the Father is an offering of his life on our behalf.

The ministry of Christ to the Father takes us into the heart of the atonement as a work of grace that belongs within the very being of Jesus Christ. By humbling himself and taking "the body of our humiliation" (Philippians 3:21), putting on the flesh that was enslaved to sin, becoming a servant, Christ has become Adam for us, rendering the flesh now capable of the Word, making us walk no longer according to the flesh but according to the Spirit. Jesus Christ in the flesh of his humanity offers himself to the Father, ministering among us and praying for us, then giving up his life as a ransom that pays the debt left by sin.

We were unable to minister these things to God for ourselves, but through the Word that was united to us we come to share by faith in his self-offering and exaltation. That which always was and is Christ's is now imparted to us. For he took our infirmities and hungers into himself and gave us in exchange what was his. As he for our sake became a man, so we for his sake are exalted.

The Wonderful Exchange

The consequence of the dual mediatorial ministry of Jesus Christ is the transition of humankind from one state into another, which the theological tradition came to call "the wonderful exchange" as a commentary on 2 Corinthians 8:9: "You know the generous act [grace] of our Lord Jesus Christ, that though he was rich, yet for your sakes he became poor, so that by his poverty you might become rich." The idea is also summed up in John 17:22: "The glory that you have given me I have given them." Out of the measureless love of God, Jesus Christ became what we are in order to make us what he is. He descended, wrote Athanasius, to effect our promotion, and made us sons and daughters of the Father. For Athanasius this is the glorious conclusion to Christ's ministry to the Father on our behalf.

The Athanasian argument turns on Christ's twofold mediatorial ministry of the things of God to humankind and of the things of humankind to God. In this dual movement Christ mediates both God to us and us to God in the unity of his incarnate personhood.

The important point for us here, and on which foundation I shall build, is Christ's vicarious humanity in the incarnation where he offers the things of humankind to God. As my teacher Thomas F. Torrance of Edinburgh University often used to say, Christ lived to bend back the will of humankind into a perfect submission to the will of God through a life lived in active filial obedience to his heavenly Father.

A Covenant Fulfilled

Let us take a respite from the rigorous theology of Athanasius to reflect on an answer to the grumpy sermon respondent who insisted on the need for his own human response to the Word of God. I am not denying that there is a place for the human response to the grace-gift of the gospel. But the response is understood in terms of a covenant already fulfilled from God's side and the human side by Jesus Christ.

The gospel is not a bilateral contract where God meets his obligations and we must meet ours or else the contract is void. Rather, our response is one of gratitude for a grace-gift given *and received* unconditionally in love, *not* the meeting of a requirement so that a grace-gift may be received. Our response is the thankful consequence of the response of Jesus Christ, who offers in our place the Amen of faith and obedience that we, in our sin, do not and cannot offer. Paul wrote, "For in him every one of God's promises is a 'Yes.' For this reason it is through him that we say the 'Amen,' to the glory of God" (2 Corinthians 1:20).

Christ believes and obeys for us. Our response is not the meeting of a contractual obligation. If it were understood in that way, the gospel would become a duty to be fulfilled and an obligation to be met. Instead we are cast back on and can rely on Christ's faithfulness, not on our own faithfulness.

No Despair

So when I have days or seasons of doubt and unfaithfulness or an attitude of lassitude concerning Christian life and ministry, I am not now thrown into despair. Rather, I trust myself to the faithfulness of Jesus, which he in his humanity continually offers to the Father on my behalf. In this way backsliding is robbed of its vicious bite. I am reminded of Paul's words "For freedom Christ has set us free" (Galatians 5:1).

To that earnest interrogator who questioned the theological validity of my sermon, I have this to say. The gospel is better news than you think. Jesus does not save you if and only if you respond. He already includes you in the blessings of his grace, in the blessings of his response, so that in him already you have new life. Now he sends you his Spirit to live that new life and enjoy it. So believe, repent, live the Christian life in Christ, in whom alone you have life.

The Key to the Kingdom?

Charles Partee, my colleague and friend at Pittsburgh Theological Seminary, is a wonderful teacher. He invents all manner of pedagogical novelties to get good (in his case, Calvin's) theology into his students' heads. One of his best is the illustration of the key.

Charles holds up a house key and tells the students that this is the key to their room in the kingdom of heaven. There are three ways they can get the key according to three different theological traditions. There is the way of medieval Catholicism: climb the upward ladder, get to the top, you get the key. Next he illustrates the perspective of

Protestant pietism. He lays the key on the table and tells the students that all they have to do is get up from their desks and come forward and pick it up. Finally he walks over to a student, puts the key in her hand and tells her to keep the room clean. That position he associates with John Calvin.

Why Bother?

By now some of you are asking, "If Jesus has done it all for me, why then should I bother?" In my teaching career I have been asked that question more than any other. I have two answers. One is dismissive, the other is serious, but I believe both are correct. The dismissive answer is this: If you have to ask the question, you don't get it. You have not yet understood what I have been saying. The serious answer explores the issue more deeply.

"Why should I bother, if Jesus has already responded for me?" As I have pondered this question through the years, I have begun to wonder if the issue is one of apperception, the framework out of which we interpret experience. For example, one person looks at a house and sees a home. Another looks at a house and sees an investment. Something very basic is going on about how we see the world or, more generally, apprehend experience.

With respect to the theological issue before us, I look at the gospel and see my response as a consequence of God's grace and love. Employing marriage analogies to make theological points is a dangerous business. The proportion between God and marriage breaks down in the face of sin. Also, not everybody is married, so we cannot make marriage normative. Nevertheless I am going to try a marriage analogy.

I am faithful to my wife. I have promised to love her unconditionally. There is nothing she needs to do to earn my love and fidelity. Similarly, she loves me unconditionally. We live within the scope of our love. She forgives me when I hurt her; likewise, I forgive her. We know there is nothing we can do to earn the other's love and acceptance. Now, within the marriage there are obligations and imperatives of behavior. But they flow from the love that is shared; they are not conditions for receiving love. Right living within marriage is an expression of freedom and joy. To ask *why* we should be faithful to one another in meeting the behavioral consequences of mutual love is simply not to understand what I am talking about. It is not to understand what a marriage is.

VICARIOUS MINISTRY

It is now time to make a major move as we turn to the second half of this chapter. I have laid the groundwork with the discussion of the vicarious *humanity* of Christ. Here I turn to think about the vicarious *ministry* of Christ, which he does in our place and in which we share. Be in no doubt, this classical theology of the church may shake us to the core by profoundly challenging our operating assumptions concerning ministry.

What is the ministry that Jesus Christ does in place of us as he ministers the things of God to us and the things of humankind to God? This is the huge question that Athanasius's development of his Christology has left us to ponder.

In the preceding chapter I wrote of Jesus Christ as the minister of the things of God to us: the grace of the Lord Jesus Christ, the love of God and the communion of the Holy Spirit. Now we cut to the chase with respect to the second part of Athanasius's dual-action Christology: the ministry of Jesus Christ in which, in our place, he responds to the Father in filial obedience and love, offering the human ministry that is acceptable to the Father and for the healing of the people. To put it differently, in the freedom of his love and by the agency of the Holy Spirit, what is it that Jesus does? Notice that the question is in the present tense!

He Prays, Teaches, Works

There is a lovely fifteen century Latin hymn, "O Love, How Deep, How Broad, How High" (trans. Benjamin Webb, 1854). The fourth verse states in its own way the ministry of Christ.

> For us he prayed, for us he taught;
> For us his daily works he wrought;
> By words and signs and actions thus
> Still seeking not himself, but us.

Christ prays, teaches and works for us. John Leith, the late Southern Presbyterian theologian, put it in conventional terms when he wrote that the renewal of the church would come about through ministries of preaching, teaching and pastoral care (*From Generation to Generation*, Westminster John Knox, 1990). At Pittsburgh Theological Seminary where I teach, there is a middler Pastoral Studies sequence over three academic periods: Christian education, pastoral care and homiletics. Allow me to expand the category of "preacher" to include "leader of worship," and we have here the basic work of ministry, long recognized and still legitimate.

In what ministry of Christ do we share when we consider the work of the minister? The New Testament understands Jesus as *leitourgos, didaskalos* and *diakonon*. He is the minister in the holy place (Hebrews 8:2), he ministers as the teacher (John 3:2) and he ministers as the one serving (Luke 22:27). Let us look at Christ as the one who leads our worship and proclaims the Word of God, who teaches us the things of God and who acts in the freedom of his love for us and for our salvation. Recognizing that Christ's ministry is not reducible to these aspects, we will let them stand in for the greater whole to make the point of the chapter.

What Makes Worship Christian?

Given the current debates over worship, the reality of Christ as minister is important for the church to realize. The terms "traditional," "contemporary" and "blended worship" are freely tossed about. Praise songs vie with hymns, worship spaces with sanctuaries, stages with chancels, casual clothes with pulpit or academic robes, ministers in pulpits with preaching from the floor. The newly minted emergent congregations have turned to a combination of art and mysticism to attract people for whom the gospel is a wholly new experience. There the mandatory marks of ministerial office have become jeans, flowing shirttails and some tasteful body piercings rather than the clerical collar and liturgical vestments.

Whatever style of worship is adopted, however the minister dresses, no matter the architecture and furnishing of the place where worship occurs, we must ask, What makes this specifically Christian worship? No expression of liturgy, style of singing, item of clothing or piece of furniture joins worshipers to Christ more than any other. Most of the fuss is over minor issues. Ministerial accouterments have always followed fashion. Anxiety arises when fashions change. The alb, for example, is a contemporary expression of late Roman underwear or nightwear! The tippet is just a medieval scarf worn in a nonheated church! There was a day when no well-placed minister would have been seen outside without wearing a wig!

Then what makes worship Christian? I have already recommended James B. Torrance's book *Worship, Community and the Triune God of Grace*. In it he argues that most worship today is functionally unitarian rather than trinitarian. By this he means our worship is centered on what *we* do. As worshipers we sing, we pray, we listen to the sermon, we take holy Communion, we pay our tithes and so on. As ministers we preach, lead the worship and pronounce the benediction. Jesus is an example, a topic and a motivation; but he plays no primary role. At best we make a vague tilt in the direction of the Holy Spirit to make it all come together.

Jesus the Minister in the Sanctuary

In contrast, Torrance suggests that the deep structure of Christian worship has a dynamic Trinitarian pattern and action. Worship is through the Son, to the Father, in the power of the Holy Spirit. That is, Jesus mediates our worship. He is *ton hagion leitourgos*, the servant of the holy things, or as the NRSV translates Hebrews 8:2, Christ is the "minister in the sanctuary." He is the one who serves in the tabernacle of the Lord. Before we worship, whether as leader or member of the congregation, Jesus is already in place as the one who ever lives to join our worship to his praise of the Father within the unity of the Godhead. As he is the Word of God who speaks himself forth, likewise he is the worshiping human respondent, hearing that Word and ministering the human response of faith and love to God.

Jesus Christ offered and continues to offer the worship that gladdens the Father's heart, the praise that is worthy and rightly due. God in, through and as Jesus Christ provides the worship that God wishes from us. Before we have arrived in church, Christ the *leitourgos*, the liturgist, has stood in for us, leading all creation's praise to the Father. Our Amen of worship is in response to and a sharing in his prior and ongoing Amen. Jesus Christ acts ahead of us and in our place as the High Priest of our confession (Hebrews 3:1).

Christ in the Lord's Supper

Let me illustrate the point this way. Conventionally we hold the view that in the Lord's Supper, Christ is mediated to us through bread and wine. As we participate in the ritual, Christ, according to one view or another, is made present for us.

Think of the Lord's Supper another way. Consider that Christ, in the freedom of his love and in the Spirit, is already present for us as the thank offering to the Father on behalf of all creation. Before the Eucharist or thank offering is consecrated, he is already the Eucharist, the thank offering on our behalf. It is the presence of the Lord who, in the consecration of the communion elements, mediates them as his body and blood. He, the thank offering, mediates the liturgical Eucharist; the liturgical Eucharist does not mediate him. He makes himself, the Eucharist, present as a witness to himself, so that when we feast on him and share in his life, we in him and he in us share in his thank offering to the Father. By this understanding the mediatorial priesthood of the church is irrelevant to the Eucharist. The only priesthood that matters is the priesthood of Christ.

Christ in the Sermon

The sermon should be understood in a similar way. The sermon does not mediate Christ; Christ mediates the sermon. Paraphrasing Karl Barth, it is not Christ who needs the sermon; it is the sermon that needs Christ. He is the living Word of God. He is practical, relevant and significant. It is not the preacher's job to invent something religiously winsome or to make Jesus connect with the lives gathered in the sanctuary. Jesus as the living Word of God is already the living sermon who is prior to any words the preacher might utter.

It is not the preacher's word that heals, blesses and announces hope or that convicts, transforms and declares forgiveness. The preacher's job is to bear witness to what the Lord is saying to the people as the Word of God. The kerygmatic task is predicated on who Jesus Christ is and what he has said and done and what he says and does. For this reason preaching is derivative work. On these terms and only on these terms, preaching is the foundation of the church's life.

What Is the Lord Saying?

The first responsibility of the preacher, to which all homiletical techniques are held accountable, is to bear witness to the one who addresses the people in his own name and authority. The hermeneutical task is to answer the question, What is the Lord saying to this people on this day? Faithful preaching is the fruit of deep theological apprehension of Jesus Christ in the context of this people at this time. You know Jesus Christ; you know this people. What is his Word to them today?

If you know the Lord and know your people, believing that he lives as the Word of God who speaks to his people his Word of grace and love, your preaching will never run dry. Of course, there will be times when discernment is obscure, for you see in glass darkly or hear in a cavern dimly. Bearing witness to him will get you into trouble, for you will be standing alongside him, and they too (the personnel committee) may come for you in the night. You will struggle to get the right words and evocative images and the compelling examples, for you are a cracked clay jar. Just remember it is not about you.

Of course ministry is hard, even deadly; but it has always been thus and always will be. Look at the best. Gregory of Nazianzus, the great theologian and bishop of Cappadocia, died in lonely retirement thinking himself a failure. John Chrysostom of Antioch, the greatest preacher of the Greek church, died in exile in a rain ditch. Gregory the Great, the reforming abbot-Pope who wrote the longest used pastoral text in the church's history, *Pastoral Care,* was dragged to the papacy on his sickbed and could only get up a few hours a day thereafter. Martin Bucer, the reformer of Strasbourg, died in exile in England, thrown out by the people among whom he had so faithfully ministered. Richard Baxter, the Puritan pastor of Kidderminster, was removed from his parish after what might be regarded as the most successful ministry ever in the Church of England.

Be of good heart and stout resolve! For Jesus is still speaking to his people. On his speaking alone you must rely. Listen, therefore, and tell them what it is you hear the Lord saying to his people: "Thus says the Lord."

"Good Sermon, Pastor"

Is there any more stupid comment about a sermon than the church-door comment "Good sermon, Pastor"? What is being said? "I approve of/enjoyed/was stimulated by what Jesus was saying this morning." By such a comment we sermon-hearers make ourselves the arbiter of the value and virtue of the Word of God.

The reverse also applies when we think it is our place to express dissatisfaction over what Jesus said and did. Certainly the preacher can get in the way of proclamation through not bearing faithful witness to what Jesus is saying to the people, through getting too much into the center of things or through muddled thinking and poor expression. Nevertheless the sermon is still not ours to control.

When the sermon bears witness to what Jesus is saying, that is entirely a miracle of God's making. The Word of God, Jesus, apart from whom there is no sermon, chooses to address his people. That is the miracle week by week on which we depend. Teach this to the people so that they grow in knowledge of the miracle of our salvation. *Deus dixit*, God speaks.

Christ the Teacher

Christ is the teacher of the things of God. He is the *didaskalos*. The Greek verb *didasko* is used ninety-seven times of Jesus and the apostles. Teaching was a major slice of their ministries. Remember our theme is that we do not mediate Jesus Christ. He mediates us. How this is to be understood with regard to the teaching ministry of the church is a special challenge, however, because in teaching we have a subject to teach: the teachings of Jesus Christ. How in teaching does Jesus Christ mediate us rather than we him?

Teaching and Feeding

I will take Mark 6: 34 as a biblical cross section to introduce the theme of Jesus as the Teacher. The setting is the first feeding story in Mark. Especially worthy of notice is the connection between the characterizations of Jesus and the crowd. Jesus has compassion on them because they are like sheep without a shepherd. The result is that he taught them many things. The parallel passage at Luke 9:11 tells us that he taught them about the kingdom of God. Notice the wilderness setting, suggesting the disciples' and the crowd's depleted spiritual condition. The setting fits in well with the need to have our ministries displaced by the ministry of Jesus.

A great crowd has gathered, interrupting the desire of Jesus and the disciples for retreat and rest. Jesus has compassion on them. The Greek verb *splanchnizomai* means "to have one's bowels turned inside out." It is a powerful experience of solidarity with the suffering of another person. The veterinary root of the word, referring to the entrails of animals, keeps us from missing the physical impact of the solidarity. It is like having a hard blow to the solar plexus.

Compassion characterizes Jesus' ministry in a special way. In this case it causes him to rearrange his priorities. The crowd certainly needs food. But Mark lays a heavy theological motif over the crowd. They are like sheep without a shepherd, and their spiritual need is given priority as the immediate focus of Jesus' compassion. The allusion is to Numbers 27:17 and Ezekiel 34:5. The crowd needs both guidance and deliverance. Jesus is the messianic Teacher and Leader of the people in their exodus through the wilderness. He is God's Davidic servant who will give them wilderness rest. The combination of teaching and feeding is a biblical sign of the breaking in of the new age of God's reign. Mark has Jesus enact what Luke names as the content of the teaching: the kingdom of God.

He Who Does, Teaches

To move from the sublime to the clichéd, there is probably some truth in the wellworn maxim that those who can, do, while those who can't, teach. Here, however, we must violate the common wisdom and insist that Jesus the *didaskalos* is to be understood as the act or *doing* of God. In Jesus' case, he who does, teaches.

John 14:6 offers a helpful framework to explore what it means that Jesus is the *didaskalos*, the teacher who mediates us to God. Jesus said "I am the way, and the truth, and the life. No one comes to the Father except through me." We can see unfolding a threefold stratified understanding where level two deepens the meaning of level one, and level three deepens the meaning of level two.

Level one: Knowing the way—what the teacher teaches →

Level two: Knowing the truth—the teacher is the one taught →

Level three: Knowing the life—through the Son, and in the Holy Spirit, we have communion with the Father.

We move from the teaching of Jesus, to Jesus the teacher who is himself the truth, to the deep knowing of God that arises from sharing in the life of God, the fruit of our union with Christ. To complicate what is already difficult enough, level three then feeds back to our grasp of level one and the process begins again in an ongoing pedagogical spiral that takes us deeper and deeper into the life and knowledge of God through Jesus Christ.

Let us now look at each level and reflect on how moving through them strengthens our grasp on what it means that Jesus is the teacher.

Level One

Teaching the teachings of Jesus does not carry much difficulty for us, for it fits easily into our notion of teaching. There is a corpus of material. It can be taught. We enquire into what Jesus taught and we reflect on what it means for our lives. This is basic Christian education at the level of Bible knowledge and application.

Of course it is not quite as easy as that! We start there but we can't stay there. Hermeneutical concerns immediately arise. What did Jesus mean, assuming that we are convinced that it was Jesus who said it? As the process of entering into the stratified structure of understanding continues, our apprehension of level one activity deepens. The teaching of Jesus moves from moral and religious instruction to an ever-deeper engagement with him as the Word of God. We are forced to deal with him not just as a religious teacher who teaches with authority, but as himself the truth of God. Processing through the three levels of understanding and allowing the process to loop back on itself like a continuing spiral, we discover that we cannot for long remain at the level of moral and religious discourse. We are forced to come to terms with who he is and what it means for us that we know him, and knowing him, know God.

Level Two

Level two, which we will discuss fully in the next chapter under the rubric of union with Christ, immediately reverses the movement of mediation. Through the work of the Holy Spirit, that is, God's act, we are brought into a profound engagement with the living Lord. We move from learning about the teachings of Jesus to actually dealing with a living Lord who draws us into union with himself to share in his life as the truth of God. At this point Christian education has taken a wholly new turn.

Most of us are familiar with the concept of a personal relationship with Jesus. The problem in common understanding is that we imagine it is something we do and over which we have control. A relationship with Jesus, rather, is his act in the freedom of his love, through the work of the Spirit, in which he binds us to share in his life as the truth of God. It is not truth as an idea, an argument or a proposition. It is truth as personal being who encounters us on his own terms by being in relationship with us. Here is knowing on a wholly new level.

Let us look briefly at some themes in the letter to the Colossians. Paul is concerned with the truth the Colossians were taught (Colossians 2:7). Teachers have come into the congregation insisting on the need for ascetical practices that lead to special knowledge necessary for the proper worship of God. Paul goes to considerable effort to decry such "philosophy and empty deceit" (Colossians 2:8). Special observances and pious practices have no merit. Christ alone is sufficient! He is the true and only mediator who takes us to the Father. "He is the image of the invisible God, the firstborn of all creation" (Colossians 1:15). "All things," a choruslike phrase that repeats through the Christ hymn, "have been created through him and for him" (Colossians 1:16). In him "all the fullness of God was pleased to dwell" (Colossians 1:19). Through him God reconciled all things on earth and in heaven (Colossians 1:20).

Colossians rightly gives pride of place to the all-sufficient Lord Christ. He is Lord of all, Lord of the cosmos. Jesus Christ the word of truth (Colossians 1:5) is rendered specific in a threefold form. First, Paul insists that Christ is all-sufficient for knowledge of and relationship with God. Nothing and no one else is required. Second, that which has separated us from God, the debt of our trespasses, has been paid off in full, nailed to the cross (Colossians 2:14). Third, alien spiritual forces at war with God have been disarmed and their shame paraded in public (Colossians 2:15). In Christ, and in Christ alone, there is the fullness of salvation. The believer can be presented to God holy, blameless and free from accusation (Colossians 1:22). This word of truth is bearing fruit and growing in the whole world (Colossians 1:6). It has been proclaimed to every creature under heaven (Colossians 1:23). The goal is to present everyone mature in Christ (Colossians 1:28).

Level Three

Communion with the Father is the end and goal of all our knowing, when we share in Christ's own knowledge of and life in God. What an amazing idea this is: knowing God through sharing in the life of God. Communion with God is the goal of Christian education.

To suggest something of what communion with the Father means through our union with Christ, I have often used the image of being enfolded into the inner life of the Trinity. We come to know God "from the inside." No longer do we know only *about* God, but we have a foresight, even in a mirror dimly, of seeing—knowing—face to face. To know Jesus through a relationship with him, which is the Spirit's work, is to share in some important sense in the Father-Son relationship. It is in some sense to participate in the life of the Trinity.

I have intentionally put a qualifier in the last two sentences. The more deeply we enter into this kind of knowing, the less we can easily speak of it with analogies and metaphors drawn from everyday experience. The transformation of our minds through knowing God (Romans 12:2) causes us to stretch language to the breaking point. As only the best of our poets and novelists can speak adequately of human love, likewise the deep knowledge of God that we share in and through Christ requires the best of the saints and hymn writers to bring it to some degree of acceptable expression. Yet it is surely true that the deep knowing of God is found in the faith that expresses its joy in believing in a countless number of congregations scattered throughout history and around the world.

Christ Serving

Christ is the one serving. According to Athanasius, Christ ministers the things of humankind to God. As the *diakonon* of Luke 22:27, in the context of the institution of Lord's Supper, Jesus tells his disciples that he is among them as the one serving. The Son does what he sees the Father doing (John 5:19). He does the will of the one who sent him (John 5:30).

The account of Jesus healing the blind beggar near Jericho illuminates the point. As Jesus approaches the city, the impoverished and desperate man shouts out for mercy. The crowd cruelly turns on him, but he shouts all the more. Jesus hears his urgent cry, has the man brought to him and then asks, "What do you want me to do for you?" (Luke 18:41). However, a caveat: don't read this as a moral tale about an attitude that needs to be born in you. The story is about Jesus' attitude of service. Leave it at that.

The Washing of Feet

The nature of the Lord's service is seen again when Jesus washes the disciples' feet at the Last Supper. Jesus says, "For I have set you an example [literally 'that which is shown'], that you also should do as I have done to you" (John 13:15). Again a caveat: it is a mistake to think that we follow this pattern of behavior only as a response to a moral command, thus imitating Christ. Christ is the one serving. Everything in our ministries depends on that. In union with Christ, the foot washing illustrates the pattern of life that ensues. In Christ we will share in his life of service, and this is what it will look like. "In Christ" is what we must explore, not the mechanics of foot washing.

The full significance of Christ as the one serving is well summed up by Paul's words "For you know the generous act of our Lord Jesus Christ, that though he was rich, yet for your sakes he became poor, so that by his poverty you might become rich" (2 Corinthians 8:9).

Look to Jesus

My appeal in this book is to weary pastors who have for too long carried the load of ministry and feel crushed by it. My friends and colleagues, you have been blighted by a theology of ministry that was long on duty and short on grace, long on what you must do and short on what Jesus has done and does for you. I invite you to turn to the *diakonon,* the one serving, for he is carrying the load of ministry for you and for the sake of the people over whom you have been placed by him in pastoral charge. It is his service they need, not yours. Only his ministry is redemptive.

As you have often preached, so I say now to you: look to Jesus, for he is the one serving. I invite you to develop the theological apperception to see what Jesus—in the freedom of his love and in the power of the Spirit—is doing among your people and to trust that the Lord has bound you to that continuing ministry.

The Lord does not call you to serve with a top up of grace now and then to help you along the way. You don't need new strategies for ministry as much as a fresh sense that you have been grabbed by the scruff of your spiritual neck by Jesus Christ. The problem is more serious than solutions rendered by ministerial first aid. The gospel is more radical than all of that. You are called to a profound *metanoia,* to a have new mind, to adopt a theology more faithful to the ministry of Jesus Christ. Abandon the theology that has brought you to this place of exhaustion and depression. Abandon *your* ministry; or if that's too hard, trust that what you are feeling is the death throes of ministry, its crucifixion. I know it is painful. But a new thing is being born in you. For he comes now to help you understand that he has joined you to himself and to what he is doing for you and your people.

4

Getting In on Christ's Ministry

Union with Christ

The subject matter of this chapter, union with Christ, may be unfamiliar to many people. Certainly one does not hear or read much discussion of its merits. Yet it was arguably John Calvin's central doctrine. I will make the case that union with Christ is a key doctrine for practical theology and the faithful practice of ministry.

This chapter will proceed by way of reflections on a number of New Testament texts. Two reflections are in the form of theological commentary and two are in homiletical style. These texts will anchor and guide the discussion as we proceed.

A Sermon: Philippians 3:12-14

Recently my wife preached a glorious sermon. I have her permission to draw on it to set up the agenda for this chapter. Her text was Philippians 3:12-14, a passage we have already come across in our reflections.

> Not that I have already obtained this or have already reached the goal; but I press on to make it my own, because Christ Jesus has

> made me his own. Beloved, I do not consider that I have made it my own; but this one thing I do: forgetting what lies behind and straining forward to what lies ahead, I press on toward the goal for the prize of the heavenly call of God in Christ Jesus. (Philippians 3:12-14)

Cathy set the sermon in the context of a television appearance by Jane Fonda to promote her autobiography, *My Life So Far.* She found Fonda to be a fragile yet winsome person who spoke of her need to be perfect and of her despair at never being good enough and deserving of love. Her despair led her into eating disorders to try to stay thin and into abusive relationships to gain acceptance. Her life was all about "Try harder. You're not yet good enough."

When we read Philippians 3:12-14, do we hear the demand to try harder as we press on to be perfect? Cathy commented at this point in her sermon that "feeling the need to be perfect, but being certain that we are not ever going to be perfect, can result in our playing the role of Happy Christian or Good Samaritan or Willing Worker or Gracious Benefactor, when in reality we are busy hiding sins of resentment, anger, doubt and despair." Christianity in these terms becomes a religion of joylessly striving to meet the demands of *shoulds* and *oughts*.

* * *

Now comes the part I want to share with you, which I cite more or less as Cathy wrote it.

I Think I Can

When I was small [she preached] one of my favorite books was *The Little Engine That Could.* It is the story of a little train engine that was dwarfed and intimidated by the larger, shinier, more powerful engines that could pull long lines of railway cars between great cities and up and down mountains. The little engine was only used to transfer cars in the railway yard from one track to another. It was a modest, unassuming little engine of quite limited aspirations.

One day, one of the great big successful engines was supposed to pull a long train full of toys over the mountain, but it broke down. How would the children on the other side of the mountain get their toys? What a crisis! The only train engine available to help was the little engine who rarely ventured beyond the railway yard. Could it possibly pull the heavy train filled with toys over a mountain?

Against all the odds the little engine decided to try. It pulled and pulled with all its might, chugging slowly up the mountain saying, "I think I can. I think I can. I think I can." What determination! What courage! It was made of sterner stuff than those other engines. "I think I can. I think I can. I think I can." What drive! What desire! It would not fail all those good little boys and girls who obviously had earned those toys. "I think I can. I think I can. I think I can." By sheer guts and willpower the little engine that could dragged that heavy train up and over the mountain. As he went down the other side, he said to himself "I thought I could! I thought I could! I thought I could!"

The story should be required reading for everyone who believes in, or who wants to inspire belief in, the Protestant work ethic. The Protestant work ethic is the ideal that urges you to pull yourself up by your bootstraps and be independent, self-supporting and self-sustaining. The Protestant work ethic was alive and well when I was growing up. You didn't even have to be a Protestant to believe in it or to feel like a guilty failure if you weren't as successful as the little engine that could. Nor did you have to be all that accomplished yourself before you could justify looking down on others who obviously weren't trying hard enough.

Of course, as a child I didn't understand all those dynamics. I just liked the story. Now that I'm a grown up theologically trained person, I can see how the story expresses something many of us accepted as a given. The way to succeed in life and be judged a good boy or girl was to focus intently on your own personal goal or mountaintop, to pull with all your might and to keep saying to yourself *I think I can. I think I can. I think I can.*

You may be wondering, *What's wrong with that?* Positive thinking might help those who feel discouraged and defeated by their circumstances in life. There is plenty in the Bible about perseverance and sticking to your calling no matter what.

Let's look more closely at what the Bible says in the text from Philippians 3. Paul acknowledges in verse 12 that he has not yet obtained *this* but is pressing on to make it his own. What is *this* that he has not yet obtained? If we back up to verses 10 and 11, we can choose from several options. There Paul speaks of the power of Christ and sharing in his sufferings. He talks about becoming like Christ in his death and about the resurrection from the dead. But the first thing Paul says in verse 10 is "I want to know Christ." The other things, such as the power, sharing of suffering, dying and resurrection, are all aspects of or results of knowing Christ.

Knowing Christ

When Paul speaks of knowing Christ, he doesn't mean that he would recognize Jesus if he passed him on the street or that he knows about Christ's life and teachings. Instead he means the intimacy of knowing and being known by the Savior. It is a relational perceiving of the person and work of Christ that is ongoing, ever-deepening and ever-widening. It means drawing closer and closer to Christ and being in communion with Christ through the Holy Spirit.

Knowing Christ is like what happens in a long-term marriage. Husband and wife continue through the years to deepen their knowing of one another, their commitment to one another, their bond with one another. That is what Paul is striving for, reaching for, pressing on to attain, this kind of knowing, this kind of living bond, this kind of intimate communion with Christ.

Running Behind Christ

In this race he is running, Paul is running behind Christ, the one he so wants to know. That is very significant, especially when you couple it with his own admission that he is in this race "because Christ Jesus has made me his own" (Philippians 3:12). Notice the indicative that here calls forth and controls the imperative. It was not his decision for Jesus that was all-important and got him running. It was Jesus' decision for him. It was God's choice of him which put him in the race. He is running behind Jesus in the slipstream of the Holy Spirit. Paul is bonded to Christ by the Holy Spirit. He is being drawn forward toward the goal by Christ himself, who has chosen to run the race for us because we cannot run this race for ourselves in our own power.

Christ Crossing the Finish Line

Contrary to the Protestant work ethic, it is not hard work, personal effort or excessive sweat that will bring us to the goal. Only Christ crossing the finish line ahead of us will draw us forward in the power of his resurrection. Paul even repeats the point when he says, "Beloved, I do not consider that I have made it my own" (Philippians 3:13). Forget about those bootstraps. The way to run this race is to follow in Christ's slipstream, to get in behind him, the perfect man, and to allow his perfection to envelop us and draw us into a saving relationship.

Hidden within our text is a subtle warning about the danger of misunderstanding the nature of pressing on. The Greek word translated "press on" has a number of meanings. *Dioko* can mean press, pursue, follow, persecute or give. The same word is used in the book of Acts in Paul's account of his conversion. When the risen Christ says to him "Saul, Saul, why do you persecute me?" (Acts 9:4) it is the same word *dioko*. Following, persecuting, pressing on—do you see the danger?

Before his conversion Paul was totally self-propelled, driven and determined to deal with Christ in his own way. He was running a race then too. It was his own race, although he thought wrongly that it was God's race. He was caught up in that perfecting obsession which was a way of life for him as a Pharisee. Then he was pressing on toward the goal with a determination to rival that of the Little Engine That Could. The work ethic of the Pharisees was not dissimilar to the Protestant work ethic. What was the result? He was persecuting Christ!

Let us beware that in our own race we do not get out ahead of Christ, doing our own thing and striving for perfection in our own terms. That way will always result in failure. We will find ourselves entangled in insidious self-destructive sins which will have to remain secret sins if we are going to maintain our facade as happy, successful Christians. That's what happens when we forget our dependence upon Christ, the forerunner and perfecter of our faith (Hebrews 12:2). We actually end up rejecting the grace that wants to pull us into the slip-stream behind Jesus.

No Easy Jog

Given the danger of misinterpretation, why would Paul use such imagery? Why use the metaphor of a race for the Christian life at all? Why emphasize the effort of pressing on, striving and straining for the goal? The fact that we run this race in the power of Christ, drawn forward by the Holy Spirit, does not mean that our life in Christ is an easy jog in the park. Our struggles with culture and with sin and with the church itself are real challenges. There is an uphill feel to this race, even though we run it in the strength of our Spirit-bound union with Christ.

Paul is being painfully honest here in describing his struggle, his faith and his hope. There are mountains to be overcome. We live in terms of a reality that is already, but not yet. Our salvation is real and it is assured, the race is won, but we are still straining to pull our not-yet-perfected-in-Christ lives over a mountain. At least, that's what it feels like. At times it feels as if the engine driving us is very little. Our faith is shaky, our willpower wavers and we get discouraged. Paul knew all of that. But he did not want us to fall back on the ethos of what we now call the Protestant work ethic, just as he didn't want himself to fall back into Pharisaism. He wants us to strive instead to know Christ and to rely on him in everything.

So we must continue our uphill race, slipstreaming in behind our Savior, letting Christ pull us forward, up and over the mountain. As we joyfully ride down the other side, anticipating a whole range of mountains spread out before us in a race that will continue for the rest of our lives, we might be heard to exclaim, "I knew he would! I knew he would! I knew he would!"

* * *

FAILED MESSIANISM

Let me put into less winsome terms what Cathy has so provocatively set before us. Union with Christ is a doctrine that bears witness to the basic fact of the Christian's life, that Jesus Christ bears the load of faithfulness on our behalf. Recall the creative slipstream image and know that he joins us to his life, his faith, his obedience and his ministry. There is no avoiding this if the Christian's life is to be understood, experienced and practiced as good news. Yet most approaches to Christian life and ministry run into a problem. At the last moment everything—faith, discipleship, ministry—is left up to us to do, as we chant the demented mantra "I think I can, I think I can, I think I can." Certainly we will invoke a little help from the Holy Spirit. But even so, the ball is now in our court. Faith becomes a matter of will; discipleship becomes a matter of obedience; ministry becomes a matter of duty.

Why is that a problem? Most of the time our own will, obedience and sense of duty will fall short of the mark. We soon fall prey to failed messianism. The Murphy's Law of the spiritual life is "If we can mess up, we will." Without Christ joining us to his own life of faithfulness, we remain stuck in the frailty of our own failed attempts at Christian faith. Such an approach becomes a recipe for guilt when we inevitably fail, or for exhaustion when, having failed, we refuse to give up and we try and try again.

Participation, Not Imitation

The Christian's life is to be understood in terms of *participatio Christi* rather than as *imitatio Christi*. We have our Christian identity and empowerment by sharing or participating in Christ's own life, which is the work of the Holy Spirit. John Calvin once called it the bond of the Holy Spirit whereby we are joined to Christ. The bond effects what Calvin then called "a mystical union" between the believer and Christ. It is because we participate in Christ's life that the New Testament call to press on makes sense as gospel for which we are grateful, rather than law, which is to be obeyed.

A Theological Commentary: Galatians 2:20

We turn now to the theologically demanding notion of Galatians 2:20, "It is no longer I who live, but it is Christ who lives in me."

Paul's statement "I, yet not I, but Christ" raises the central point: God has set forth in the person of Jesus Christ the union of God and humankind by which we may be united to God through the action of the Holy Spirit. This union we come to know by faith.

By his descent in the flesh, Christ has union with us through his assumption of our humanity into himself; this might be called the objective aspect of union with Christ. It is something God does to us. Union with Christ is subjectively actualized in us through the gift of his Spirit. It is something God does in us. So we must say at once that Christ is in us and that we are in Christ, for they complement and interpenetrate each other.

Theological tradition calls the reality we are discussing *union with Christ*. It is through this union that we partake of the blessings of his holy and obedient life. Calvin called it a real and substantial union, and it is the ground subsequently of our sharing in the benefits of Christ, especially his justification, sanctification and regeneration. However, we cannot remain justified, sanctified and regenerated without also sharing in Christ's ministry from the Father for the sake of the world. Through our communion with Christ's human nature, we in fact share in the divine life and ministry given for the world in, through and as the man Jesus.

Unbreakable Union

As I sit here writing, as you sit in your chair reading, the truth of our beings in the deepest way possible is that we are sharing in the life of God. To use an inadequate spatial metaphor, the union drives us upward and outward in the dual action of grace. Everything else in our Christian lives flows from our participation in Christ, which is the Spirit's gift.

Our unbreakable union with Christ is the defining, operative mark of the Christian's life and of the church's identity and purpose. It is the necessary and actual condition for a Christian or the church to exist in the first place. The conclusion is irresistible: there is only one ministry, that of Jesus Christ, to which through union with Christ we are joined. The Holy Spirit constitutes us, and thereby the church, in union with its Head, joining us to Christ to share *in his communion with* the Father and *in his mission from* the Father by bearing faithful witness to him in the world.

On this ground the doctrine of union with Christ is properly understood to be the central organizing feature of all Christian faith and life. It is a basic belief in the act of God that influences every other belief and every act of faith. In all things we stand before God not on the strength of our own piety, faith, good works or knowledge. Rather, because the Holy Spirit joins us to Jesus Christ, we share in everything that is his. In and through him we are children of the heavenly Father, sharing in his own life in and before and from God. Christian faith and life mean no less than this! We stand before God in Christ's name alone. We worship in Christ's name alone. And we serve in Christ's name alone.

The Radical Center

Everything in this book so far may be summed up as the theological intent of Galatians 2.20, "I, yet not I, but Christ." It is the radical center of all practical theology. It is the message of (1) the vicarious humanity and ministry of Christ and (2) our union with Christ whereby we participate in his humanity and ministry is the gospel on which we rely.

In Jesus Christ, writes Thomas F. Torrance, all human responses "are laid hold of, sanctified and informed by his vicarious life of obedience and response to the Father. They are in fact so indissolubly united to the life of Jesus Christ which he lived out among us and which he has offered to the Father, as arising out of our human being and nature, that they are *our responses* toward the love of the Father poured out upon us through the mediation of the Son and in the unity of the Holy Spirit" (*The Mediation of Christ* [Grand Rapids: Eerdmans, 1984], p. 108). So singular is the efficacy of the vicarious humanity of Christ and of our union with him that they invalidate and actually make impossible all other ways of response. In other places Torrance called it the theological equivalent of Fermat's principle in natural science, in which the selection of one way invalidates other ways.

Our Faltering Worship

What does union with Christ mean for our practice of Christian faith? Jesus acts in our place from within the humanity of our unfaithfulness, giving us a faithfulness in which we may share. He is both the truth of God and a human being keeping faith. Through our union with Christ, our faith is grounded objectively yet personally in the One who believes for us. Our faith depends upon the faithfulness of God in Christ for us. We are summoned to believe, but in such a way that we are cast back upon his faithfulness, not our own. We do not rely on our own believing but on Christ's faith on our behalf.

Likewise with regard to worship, Jesus Christ has embodied for us the response to God in such a way that henceforth all worship and prayer is grounded in him. All approach to God is in the name and significance of Jesus Christ, in which we rely on his communion with the Father. Christ has united himself to us in incarnation and us to himself in Pentecost, all in such a way that he gathers up our faltering worship into himself. In presenting himself to the Father he presents also the worship of all creation to share in his own communion with the Father.

Not a Separate Ministry

As the Son is sent from the Father, so the being of the church involves a sharing in the mission of Jesus Christ from the Father for the sake of the world. In union with Christ we are at once devoted to God and devoted to the ministry of God in the world. (This is a slightly amended form of a statement made by John McLeod Campbell, arguably Scotland's greatest theologian, in *The Nature of the Atonement,* 1856.) The ministry of the church is not another ministry different from or separate from the ministry of Christ. The ministry of the church takes its essential form and content from the servant-existence and mission of Jesus.

Today the present ascended ministry of the vicarious humanity of Jesus Christ and the ministry of the Spirit joining us to Christ's present ministry are largely lost to ministers' experience. The loss has two consequences: (1) the collapsing of ministry into a response to the moral influence of Jesus and (2) the reduction of ministry to programs, strategies and techniques that are theologically ambiguous. When the continuing and present ministry of Jesus Christ is lost, we are cast back on our own resources, and ministry becomes what we do.

Radical Thinking

Thinking radically in the light of Galatians 2:20 involves thinking through what it means that Jesus' faith, worship and ministry are the grounds of our faith, worship and ministry. Two brief observations arise, the first theological and the second pragmatic.

First, I note the danger of a slide into antinomianism. When so much is cast onto Jesus Christ, we must stay aware that faith, worship and ministry are still called for. The imperative of discipleship is not canceled by the sheer power and grace of the divine indicative. Our responses are by the Spirit. It is on Jesus' faith, worship and ministry that we rely, not on our own. We rightly affirm and call for the human *Amen* to our Lord's vicarious Amen. In all things we can and must say, "I, yet not I, but Christ."

Second, I have found through the years that this is very difficult material to teach. Not only is it conceptually demanding, but there is something counter-intuitive about it. A good student may come to apprehend the argument. More elusive is the deep conversion of mind, will and heart where we know the inner reality of being laid hold of by Christ in the Spirit, so we share in his active obedience to, communion with and mission from the Father. From my observation it requires the pains of ministry in midcareer to prepare a person for the radical transformation of "I, yet not I, but Christ."

A Sermon: Galatians 4:6

Do you ever make New Year's resolutions? This year I will . . . lose weight, get more exercise; get out of bed an hour earlier and learn Swahili. Of course none of it ever happens. The best intentions in the world lie in ruins by mid-January.

In Scotland, where we always get to the heart of things, the New Year is brought in with great celebrations. As a youngster I remember New Year's Eve, Hogmanay we call it. It is the biggest holiday of the year, well outdoing Christmas for thoroughgoing festivities. We have a custom called first-footing. It seemed as though the whole of my home town of Edinburgh, half a million people, were on the streets going in and out of each other's houses, many carrying the usual accoutrements containing amber liquid! New Year's Eve and New Year's Day are great occasions. Whenever Scots greet one another for the first time in the New Year, they shake hands and reintroduce themselves to one another. *It's a new year. I'm a new person. I can start over again. So let me introduce this new person to you.*

Americans making New Year's resolutions are as foolish as Scots each year reintroducing themselves to each other. None of it is true. I knew a preacher whose tagline was "We don't really change; we just find more and more clever reasons for staying the same." A piece of doggerel has some poignant truth: "I wish I could be what I wanted to be, before I became what I am." We continue in the same old habits, the same old frustrations, the same old excuses for not turning some part of our lives around, the same old sins, the same old routines. It's as if they are all hardwired into our brains. They are etched so deeply that we cannot find the energy or wit or will to change.

God Entered Our Stuckness

Change is hard. Making big changes that matter is even harder. We might even somewhat enjoy our little bad habits! That's why God gave us the gospel.

If it's up to us to change so that God will welcome us, we have no chance. When the Word became flesh and dwelt among us full of grace and truth, he entered into the heart of our fallen and depraved humanity. We can say he entered into our *stuckness*. God came to us at our worst and made his home there. God loved us at our wickedest, and as the man Jesus he bent our human hearts, minds and wills back into communion with God.

Our plight was hopeless. No amount of New Year's resolutions, pious good intentions or attempts to drag our moral and spiritual lives Godward was ever going to amount to anything. Where we were complete, abject and utter failures, God moved. God in Christ entered the direst deep pit of corruptible humanity. Christ laid hold of lost humankind in order to offer us "holy and blameless before him in love" (Ephesians 1:4).

God Sent His Son

We need to try to grasp how radical all this is! Paul wrote that "we were enslaved to the elemental spirits of the world" (Galatians 4:3). That is fancy biblical language. It means we were in bad shape spiritually and morally. *Enslaved* is strong word. We had no right to liberty and no hope of freedom.

For biblical and theological reasons I judge real human freedom to be a myth. Outside of God acting in the gospel, there is no freedom. We may have superficial freedoms in political and economic structures. We can vote for Mr. Bush or Mr. Kerry, or for higher or lower taxation. We can make choices between Pepsi or Coke, Ramada Inn or Holiday Inn, steak or fish. But in the hidden heart of human beings there is only darkness brought on by enslavement to the demonic powers of antichrist.

In this context we read of the glorious response of God. "God sent" (Galatians 4:4) not because we were good, pious or loving, but because God wanted us for himself and we were in no condition to respond. There was no longer any human capacity for God. That is why God sent!

God sent whom? "God sent his Son, born of a woman, born under the law" (Galatians 4:4). God sent himself. God became as we are: born of a woman, born under the law. That's what the Simeon and Anna stories in Luke are about. The demands of religious obedience are fulfilled, not by us but for us, as through the instrumentality of Mary and Joseph the baby Jesus fulfills the religious demands of the law.

God sent. The light comes into the darkness. The hope comes into no-hope. The Creator-Word comes to his own who do not know him. He comes as he always came, unconditionally and unilaterally, on his own terms and according to his own timetable. The *fullness of time* (Galatians 4:4) is more than tick-tock time. It is God's time, the time of God's own choosing. *God sent.*

He was born to the poorest of the poor, an unmarried peasant girl. Without a sanctified imagination, I doubt that western persons have the sensibility to see that here, now, in this manger, a cosmic war is being fought over us. It is the love of God versus the evil of the devil, as Martin Luther used to see it. Victory will be achieved only when the death of Jesus means the death of the worst that evil can throw at him because he is raised on the third day.

A Genuine Liberation

God sent in order to redeem and buy back those whose debt is too overwhelming to ever pay back. It is a genuine liberation. We who are alienated from our birthright have a new hitherto unavailable future. Instead of being free men and women, we were all slaves in thralldom to the rudimentary power of darkness. So *God sent* to redeem or buy us back from the evil, from its power over us, from our hopeless state.

God sent *his Son.* Paul immediately jumps to the consequence: "In order to redeem those who were under the law, so that we might receive adoption as children" (Galatians 4:5). The Greek word translated "adoption" is made up from two words which literally mean "a son" and "a placing." Because God sent his Son, we who were in bondage to elemental spirits, without a home or a family or a name, are now placed on account as if we are sons and not slaves.

The New Revised Standard Version, which I quote throughout this book, translates the Greek as "child" and "children," and I think loses the thread as a result. The Greek is "son" and "sonship." Even the Greek word *adoption* literally means "being placed as a son." The entire passage in Greek is in part a play on the word *huos—son.* This is not sexist language. It is about our receiving a relationship that comes from God and is entirely God's doing. The passage and the word play tell us that in Christ we have a theological identity as well as being sons and daughters by birth. Outside of sharing in Jesus' divine sonship we have no access to God as God's beloved and no ground for knowing that we belong in God's family.

God Sent the Spirit

Because we, men and women, are in Christ Jesus, sharing in his life and belonging to God just as his Son Jesus belongs to God, sharing therefore in his Sonship, *God sent* again. This is a second sending. "God has sent the Spirit of his Son into our hearts, crying, 'Abba! Father!'" (Galatians 4:6). We can cry out the holy name of God. We are no longer slaves but members of God's family, calling on God by his name. Now we have a Father in heaven. John Calvin said of this that it is not what persons themselves believe in the foolishness of the flesh but what God declares in their hearts.

God Cries Out to God

Notice it is God who cries out to God! God sent his Spirit so when we cry out "Abba! Dear Father!" it is God crying out to God through the instrumentality of our vocal cords. It is God naming God within the spiritual incapacity of our humanity. We can't even be trusted to speak the name of God, so God does it for us, but in our own voices. When that God-generated cry "Abba, dear Father" escapes from our lips it is the guarantee, the sure warranty, the truth, that we are members of God's family.

Only the dear Son of God can call God Father, for only he is God's Son. Because we now share in his sonship in union with him, that which is uniquely and singularly his is now given to us. What he can call the Father by name, we by the Spirit of the Son, thereby in union with him, also can, indeed must, call God. Even our response to God is made by God.

The Reformer John Knox of Edinburgh wrote that Jesus Christ is our mouth by whom we speak to God. Knox probably had Galatians 4:6 in mind. To speak God's name is the assurance that we are adopted into God's intimate fellowship, into God's family. That is the practical significance of union with Christ for the life of prayer. It is summed up in what we call the Lord's Prayer. It's not our prayer. It's Jesus' intimate prayer to the One whom he named as Father. He could pray, "My Father, who art in heaven." Because we are members of God's family through our union with Christ, we can pray his prayer as our own: "Our Father, who art in heaven."

Our Adoption Is Secure

No matter how many New Year's resolutions we break or how weak and wavering our spiritual life becomes, the deed of adoption is secure because it was enacted by God's choice and faithfulness. God sent his Son to earth. Even our response to God has already been made for us by God. Because we are joined to that response, we too can say with joy and confidence, "God sent the Spirit of his Son into our hearts crying, 'Abba! Dear Father!'"

So be of good heart, have faith, and trust that you are eternally secure in God's choice of you as the subject of his eternal love. Trust that you are in union with Christ, joined to share in his Sonship. Live in this freedom, for you are no longer a slave but a cherished member of the family, able now to speak God's name. It was all God's choice and act. You are an heir of the kingdom of God with all the rights and privileges belonging thereto. This is an inheritance that will never fade. This is what union with Christ means.

A Theological Commentary: John 15:1-11

I am a transplanted Scot who has lived in the United States since 1978 yet still carries a British passport. Sometimes I feel emotionally homeless. I don't quite belong here, and over there is no longer what I left. Maybe the reason I have preached on John 15:1-11 more than any other passage in the New Testament is that it tells me where my home is, where I belong, and I delight in the climax of sharing in Christ's joy.

> I am the true vine, and my Father is the vine grower. . . . Abide in me as I abide in you. Just as the branch cannot bear fruit by itself unless it abides in the vine, neither can you unless you abide in me. . . . Apart from me you can do nothing. . . . My Father is glorified by this, that you bear much fruit and become my disciples. (John 15:1, 4, 5, 8)

Where do I abide? I rejoice that I abide in Christ. I will go so far as to say that in some sense I am grateful for my homelessness. I don't carry the baggage of overwrought patriotism or nationalism. I can get sentimental about Scotland but, at least on my clearheaded days, I don't identify it as the chosen land. There is a sense in which my peripatetic life in which I belong neither to Scotland nor the United States has made me a good candidate for finding deep, emotionally satisfying and theologically legitimate meaning in the idea of having my home in Christ.

ENGRAFTED INTO THE VINE

John 15:1-11 employs an organic metaphor which reveals a different side of the meaning of union with Christ. Here the image is of being engrafted by the Father into the central vine, Jesus Christ, so we take our being, identity and nourishment entirely from him. Once again the image is radical. One cannot be partially engrafted. It is all or nothing. Also one can't be generically engrafted. It is a particular vine to which we are engrafted. Jesus says, "I am the true vine" (John 15:1).

A point must be made that is true in theology and the spiritual life as it is true in horticulture. A branch can't engraft itself. The vine grower makes the graft; the branch thereafter lives from the life of the vine. We mature in the spiritual life by being a grafted-onto-Christ person. Our job is to live who we are made to be by God's act of attachment. In Paul's familiar words, we live "in Christ," a phrase he used in some form 164 times!

HEALTHY FRUITBEARERS

Apart from the vine we are dead, fruitless branches fit only for burning. Yet attached to the vine we are fruitbearers. If the vine and the graft are healthy, the branch cannot be other than a fruitbearer. Attached to Christ, in union with Christ, we will bear fruit. Others will know we are Christians because we are a fecund people. There are no go-it-alone and fruitless Christians. It is the vine's ministry that is fruitful and redemptive, not the ministry of the branches in their own right. In fact apart from the vine, the branches are fit only for being gathered up and burned.

Jesus said, "Apart from me you can do nothing" (John 15:5). There is an unambiguous lack of wiggle room for human autonomy in ministry. Ministry is not a matter of a minister working hard, preaching relevant sermons, being a super-efficient congregational administrator, attending those who are sick, downcast, grieving and lonely, all the while growing the congregation and charming the people with a winsome and attractive ability to relate warmly. Outside of abiding in Christ, *we have no ministry.* It matters not how full our pastoral tool bag is and how much energy we bring to the tasks of ministry. We can do nothing apart from Christ.

What Obligations?

Given that we are engrafted onto the vine and are in union with Christ, what obligations face us? What does union with Christ mean for what we are to do?

Thomas Merton, the late American Trappist monk and spiritual writer, wrote in his classic book *New Seeds of Contemplation,* "How does an apple ripen? It sits in the sun." That was Merton's metaphor for Christian piety. We are to abide in, rest in and have our home deeply in Christ. It is that easy! We are to be who we are, not to live a lie pretending we are someone different. Try to be someone else or try to live the Christian life in a manner other than being engrafted onto Christ, and a fiery disaster awaits us.

One of the most difficult aspects of piety is learning that in a sense there is nothing we need to do. No amount of spiritual experience will get us more connected to the vine. No virtue will bring us any more into union with Christ than we are already.

The only issue is for us to attend with utter seriousness to what it means to be who we are in union with Christ. Living into our true identity in Christ means the crucifixion of the old self-justifying self. We will discover that living who we are, as opposed to living apart from Christ, involves transformation of mind *(metanoia),* conversion of the natural will and amendment of life.

We must tread carefully here. At this point Christian spirituality has had a tendency toward negativity. The old word is *mortification,* dying to self and prowling around looking for a cross to bear. So much classical Christian spirituality is bathed in seeming self-hatred.

We are in union with Christ. This is God's unilateral act of love, mercy and grace. We belong to God because Jesus has claimed us as part of himself. I don't mean to be soppy, but it's true: we can and should deeply love ourselves because we are unilaterally and unconditionally loved by God. That is where we start. There is no place for self-hatred.

Transformation, Conversion, Amendment

Attending to who we are as engrafted-onto-Christ people brings challenges. As I have already noted, three important areas require our attention: transformation of mind, conversion of will and amendment of life.

1. *Transformation of mind.* Wrong thinking concerning God leads to confusion in Christian life and ministry. If we think wrongly about God, then we get life and ministry wrong. Maturity in Christ involves developing theological acuity. High on the list of gifts that ministers can give their congregations is their commitment to be serious theologians. I don't mean getting a Ph.D. I mean commitment to the work of knowing God more and more fully. The minister is to be a student of God who through study and prayer enters deeply into the mystery of Jesus Christ as God's salvation. Theology is hard work and we will meet temptations to take shortcuts through the jungle of confusion. The truth is there is no way one can faithfully preach Jesus Christ as Lord without an ongoing transformation of mind.

2. *Conversion of the will.* Getting the arguments right is a lot easier

than getting rid of desires and motivations for action that are less than Christian. Processes of nurture and accountability that really get to the core issues of desire and motivation are notoriously difficult to identify. We have remarkable ability to construct rationalizations and put on blinders that obscure our moral vision. In addition we meet the attacks of the evil one, who seems to know our vulnerabilities better than we do. In response we must be intentional in clearheaded will awareness, guarding our eyes and ears, disciplining our imaginations, while putting before ourselves literature and art that builds us up. Our wills are pliable and need to be guided and guarded all along the way. The work of the maturation of the will is a daily task.

I have a friend who is an extremely well-known spiritual teacher and writer. He does not have a television in his house, and I suspect he is not on the Internet. Given who you are, what do you need to attend to in order to guard and guide your will so that you mature more fully in Christ?

3. *Amendment of life.* We must give attention not only to the internal areas of life. There is also the matter of private and public behavior. I have found through the years that I drive differently when I am wearing a clerical collar! Bad driving and rude driving are an offense to the gospel, especially when I am identified as a minister, because they are disrespectful and dangerous. Bad driving may not be the worst sin. But I wonder what it would mean to engage in every aspect of behavior as if I were in public wearing a clerical collar. We do all things before the eyes of God. We should not take this fact as a threat but as a positive encouragement to "do justice, and to love kindness, and to walk humbly with your God" (Micah 6:8).

In the next chapter we turn to the actual practice of ministry. We will consider our participation in the singular ministry of Jesus Christ to the glory of God and for the sake of the world.

5

Having Hitched a Ride

Ministry Today

I WAS SETTLING DOWN TO BEGIN THIS CHAPTER when a former student called inviting me to speak at a regional gathering of ministers in her denomination. When I asked about the subject matter, she launched into a brief but intense and somewhat self-righteous characterization of her pastoral colleagues, who apparently don't know what pastoral work amounts to, don't visit their people and have lost their way connecting theology to what they do or don't do day after day. I am supposed to fix that in one lecture!

Here is the issue: What is a minister supposed to do all day?

First Day on the Job

In November 1979 I was installed into the only congregation I have served as minister. It was a small semirural community just outside Pittsburgh, Pennsylvania. The congregation had no secretary, no office and very little program.

I recall with some amusement my first day on the job. My wife and I had moved our bits and pieces of furniture into the manse, and I had set up my home study with my books around me. Just after 9:00 a.m. on Monday morning I walked into the study wearing a clerical collar and a dark suit. I went to the desk, sat down and asked myself, *What do I do now?* I sat there for quite a while feeling slightly foolish and with not a clue how to fill my day. I had four university degrees, I had studied with some of the best theologians, and I hadn't a clue what to do on my first day on the job other than to sit at my desk like a clerical mannequin.

Events soon took over. I discovered someone was in hospital, a volunteer needed to know my sermon details for Sunday so she could type the bulletin, and a middle-aged somewhat shut-in member called to insist that I had to make her a pastoral visit that afternoon. She later complained to my church board that I had not prayed with her. I was not only clueless; I was also totally intimidated by her.

For the next three and a half years with these wonderful, mostly tolerant people of the Hebron Presbyterian Church, Clinton, Pennsylvania, I muddled along trying to learn my trade as a minister. Then in 1983, mercifully for them, I was called to the faculty of Pittsburgh Theological Seminary to teach, of all things, pastoral theology and pastoral care. Still I did not have a clue what a minister was supposed to do day by day, though I had read more books on pastoral theology than anyone should need to read and had even written a doctoral dissertation on the subject.

A Sorry State of Muddle

From the beginning of my ministry I have known that the discipline of pastoral theology has largely lost its way, finding its identity in pastoral counseling theories and practices. Consequently, while a lot that was helpful was learned, the practice of pastoral care was flailing around in what I would call atheological confusion. I was very early aware that the whole discipline would need to be recast. Not only pastoral care but ministry in general seemed to me to be in a sorry state of muddle.

Many years later I have focused the problem with a question: What makes pastoral work Christian? To put it otherwise, what does pastoral work look like in view of the descent of grace, who is Jesus Christ, into our midst, and to whose continuing life we are joined so as to participate in his present ministry?

The answer must be worked out, somewhat tautologically of course, in terms of the fact that it has to do with union with Jesus Christ and therefore with everything that he is about. The Theological Declaration of Barmen, written by the Confessing Church in Germany in 1933, has a wonderful statement: "Jesus Christ, as he is attested for us in Holy Scripture, is the one Word of God which we have to hear and which we have to trust and obey in life and in death." From the same decade in Germany come these simple words of Dietrich Bonhoeffer: "The other person must deal with Christ if he [or she] is to be helped" (*Spiritual Care*, trans. Jay C. Rochelle [Philadelphia: Fortress, 1985], p. 36). I doubt the issue can be put any more clearly.

The One Ministry That Saves

This small book has been about the task of answering the question of the Christian identity of pastoral ministry. I want to get as concrete as I can and ask, What then is the minister supposed to do day by day? Certain familiar theological caveats constrain our answer. Let me repeat the key affirmations. There is only one ministry, the ministry of God for us in, through and as Jesus Christ. Only Christ's ministry is redemptive in any theologically substantial sense of the term. When we try to get our ministry into the center of things, that ministry must be crucified. The good news is that by the grace and agency of the Holy Spirit we are united with the living, acting Jesus Christ. Henceforth we are graced to participate in his ministry, which is the one ministry that saves.

The Identity and Practice of Ministry

The inquiry into the identity of ministry as *Christian* is necessarily doctrinal insofar as doctrine is the church's reflection on Christ clothed with his gospel. There is content to the gospel. The content is Jesus Christ, who is the ministry of God with and for us. The practice of ministry as *Christian* is the theological act of sharing in this practice of God in certain specific regards. To put it differently, our task is to locate the identity and practice of ministry in the pattern and event of Trinitarian activity as the Word/Acts of God, Father, Son and Holy Spirit. What this means explicitly is the subject that we now explore.

I will not now turn to practical hints and helps. They are available in numerous other places. Rather, my concern is with ministry as theological praxis, as a theological act in which, through union with Christ, we participate in Christ's ministry. To that end I will shortly share the content of pastoral work as theological praxis. Before we get to that, I need to say a few words about our own formation in Christ.

We cannot share in Christ's ministering the things of God to us and of humankind to God (the formulation given by Athanasius of Alexandria) without careful attention to the disciplines of life and faith that arise from our union with Christ. Mindful that Christ said "apart from me you can do nothing" (John 15:5), we are bidden to take heed of the imperative/indicative relation embedded in John 15:4: "Abide in me as I abide in you."

There is an intrinsic connection between fruitful ministry and personal prayer, Scripture study, common worship, especially attendance at Holy Communion (Calvin made a very strong affirmation of union with Christ as the special fruit of the Lord's Supper), the practice of sharing in Christian community and so on. One has only to cast one's mind back to the piety of the greatest pastors of times past to see this connection lived out in practice.

From the early church, "Flight to Pontus" (*Oration* 2 c. 380s) by

Gregory of Nazianzus and *Pastoral Care* (590) by Gregory the Great stand as classical texts to guide ministerial piety and practice. Both texts are available in English. The English Puritan Richard Baxter's *The Reformed Pastor* remains essential reading if we would be well guided in the relation between piety and ministry. Baxter's book is a sustained pastoral theological reflection on Acts 20:28: "Keep watch over yourselves and over all the flock, of which the Holy Spirit has made you overseers, to shepherd the church of God that he obtained with the blood of his own Son." From a century ago the readily accessible books of the South African pastor Andrew Murray are recommended. There he draws out in clear convicting ways the relation of the priestly ministry of Christ, personal holiness and the work of ministry. In contemporary times the unparalleled work of Eugene Peterson draws the connections between piety and ministry with rare consistency, eloquence and insight.

Come Back to Prayer

Friends, come back to your prayer desks and absent yourselves for a while from your office desks. Recommit yourselves again (and again!) to seasons of prayer and biblical and theological study. Train the heart and mind in the ways of God. Pray to find a spiritual companion to aid you in discerning the delight of God for your life and ministry. Invite this person to encourage you in happy obedience. Left to our own devices we will most likely stumble on the bruising stones of spiritual sloth and carelessness. Practice Sabbath rest, for most likely you are tired. Practice, too, the discipline of attention to marriage and baptismal vows; take lots of time with those whom you love most closely.

In sum, I encourage you to draw creatively from the deep well of available resources in the devotional life. After all, if we have no life in Christ, we have no ministry. It was Henri Nouwen who once said that we cannot minister in the name of God if we are not living into the name of God.

Participation Past, Present and Future

Now let us turn to reflection on the practice of ministry. Core Christology affirms that Christ comes as the Word/Act of God and hears and responds as word/act of humankind. There is a past completed, a continuing and a future aspect to the work of Jesus Christ. Christ lived out the gospel of salvation through incarnation and atonement. He lived his life as the human person who is righteous before God. Thus we reflect on the whole sweep of the ministry of Jesus from his birth through his death, resurrection and ascension. But as I have insisted throughout, Christ also comes from the Father and in the power of the Holy Spirit to join us to himself to share in his present communion with the Father and in his continuing mission from the Father. This is the reality represented by the doctrine of union with Christ. Christian faith affirms further that Christ will come again to gather all things to himself and give them to the Father. Through union with Christ, which is the principal work of the Holy Spirit, we participate in Christ's ministry, attesting with thanksgiving what he did two thousand years ago, bearing witness in power to what he does today and anticipating in hope his future ministry. In ministry we recapitulate the faith of the historic ecumenical church, confessing the ministry of Jesus Christ (1) in his incarnation and atonement, in which he was present in the flesh; (2) in his ascension and reign, in which he is present in and through the Holy Spirit; and (3) in his parousia, when he comes again to bring to completion the great work of salvation.

Because pastoral work is a form of theological and christological praxis, this means that every pastoral event is constrained by the ministry of Jesus Christ.

THE JOINING OF TWO STORIES

Let me introduce you again to Mrs. Smith, whom we first encountered in chapter two. She is a godly woman, and she is elderly and does not get out much any more. Imagine it is 2:00 p.m. on a Thursday afternoon and you are about to ring the bell to her apartment in the sheltered living complex where she lives. As you press the bell, allow this question to arise: Theologically, what is about to happen over the next hour or so?

The one mistake we must not make is to assume that we bring Jesus with us. When we walk into her room I take it to be axiomatic that Jesus, in the freedom of his love and in the power of the Spirit, is already present to and with Mrs. Smith. The issue for us is to discern what he is up to in the specific context of that person on that day amid her life's circumstances.

We know our parishioner Mrs. Smith; we know Jesus the living Lord and of his abiding in her. The connection to be made between this dual knowing defines the task of pastoral ministry. At its core, pastoral work involves bearing witness to the joining of two stories, the parishioner's and God's. Who is Jesus Christ specifically for this person amid the particularities and exigencies of her current life experience? The priority of the Who? question is not only a matter of theological method; it is now the central concern of pastoral praxis.

Pastoral work is a work of theological praxis in this immediate context on the ground of who Jesus Christ is and what he did, does and will do for Mrs. Smith. How can it be explicitly Christian otherwise? The pastoral question is always to discern the Lord's actual ministry in any given situation.

THE ACTUAL MINISTRY OF GOD

The church's ministry is a participation in Christ's ministry. It is not something new of the church's invention to meet some present need or circumstance. It is not a vague imitation of Jesus Christ or the adoption of an ethical Christ principle doomed to failure because we are not messianic. It is not an ideal ministry yet to be made practical. It is the actual ministry of God which makes the church's ministry possible, practical, relevant and appropriate.

The actuality of Christ's ministry is prior to and constrains the possibility of our ministries. This is a *God*-actualized approach in contrast to a *self*-actualized and needs-responding approach. There is always the danger that a pragmatic impulse will take over under the felt ministerial pressure of meeting needs. In that case human experience and analysis of pain rather than Jesus Christ will set the agenda. Then the profoundly practical theological grounding for ministry is lost and we are back with the old problem of ministry validated by successful works.

In ministry people should expect to meet Jesus. Our task is to think through the content and meaning of our participation in the apostolic priesthood of Jesus Christ in its past, present and eschatological dimensions in such a way that the shape of ministerial practice becomes clear in concrete ways. The issue is the locus or place of Christ's apostolic priesthood (see Hebrews 3:1) in the world today. That is the truth of our life because Christ is in us and works through us, and we are in him.

Announce the Love of God

It is time now to move toward putting some flesh onto our ministries as a form of theological praxis. In view of our union with Jesus Christ, what is ministry concretely today at 2:00 p.m. on this Thursday afternoon, given the full work of Jesus Christ for Mrs. Smith?

First, all pastoral work begins within the framework and announcement of the love of God, for "God is love" (1 John 4:8). The gospel begins from the standpoint that "God so loved the world"

(John 3:16). We must first approach people not with God's judgment or even with God's forgiveness. We cannot assume that a person knows who the God is who judges or forgives him or her. Instead we come announcing and bearing the love of God.

God's love is neither some vague and pleasing affective or ethical attribute of a distantly benevolent God, nor is it a liberal philosophical counterpoint to the scholastic God of judgment and anger. God's love has its specific content precisely and actually in the fact of Jesus Christ, and thereby has a uniqueness, singularity and particularity.

Thus the first pastoral movement of the ministry of grace must be quite simply (although of immense significance) the announcement "Jesus Christ is Lord, and this Jesus who is God loves you." The statement stands over and against all other claims to divinity and all other definitions of deity. The claim is made that this man who died on the cross of Golgotha, and this man only, is the revelation of God and the event of the love of God for us. It is the announcement of the human reality as St. Paul saw it: "for you have died, and your life is hidden with Christ in God" (Colossians 3:3). God's love in Jesus Christ means that we have been claimed by God. Now nothing "will be able to separate us from the love of God in Christ Jesus our Lord" (Romans 8:39). The first pastoral act of our participation in the ministry of the grace of God is this announcement in word or act: "Jesus Christ is Lord. Jesus who is God loves you."

Care for the Person

Second, love is made actual in a pastoral sense by the quality of relationship with a parishioner. Here I gather all the skills that make for relationship: listening, acceptance of feelings, warmth of engagement, openness toward another, presence and attentiveness, taking time, affirmation, transparency and so on. No matter what your theological skills, if you do not know how to relate to another person, your pastoral work will not get off square one. After all, we are dealing with people. Knowing how people feel, how families are complex systems, how relationships can work therapeutically and so on are grist to the pastoral mill. Our knowledge and skills are very important even though I do not regard them to be definitive of pastoral care. In ministry we deal with people, and we have no choice but to be competent psychologists to some extent.

The ministry of the love of God is made actual in, through and as the whole ministry of Jesus Christ, but it is pressed through the prism of God's will and power to meet an actual person or circumstance at the point of need for grace, that is, for Jesus Christ. This is not the same as finding human needs and meeting them. It is rather the act of God to and for the person in the specificity of life's circumstance. The answer to the question Who is Jesus Christ now, here, for Mrs. Smith? must control the practice of pastoral care for her.

Theological discernment is the primary skill we need. Regardless of our therapeutic skills, without theological discernment pastoral care does not happen. God undoubtedly will be up to something, but it will be in spite of us if we are not focused on the present ministry of Jesus Christ. This is surely the meaning of John 15:5 for pastoral work: "Apart from me you can do nothing."

I identify three essential aspects of pastoral work in union with Christ: bearing witness, interpretation and symbolic action. To get these points into my students' heads I sometimes have them chant the threefold form of pastoral work.

Bear Witness to Christ

"Hey, preacher, what do you do all week?" If I am called "preacher," what do I do to pass the rest of the time? I suggest that preaching is not just an occasional task but is the center of everything we do.

If I had to choose, I would much prefer to be called "preacher" than "pastor." I am a pastor because I preach; I don't preach because I am a pastor. The church's primary and indeed defining task is to bear witness to Jesus Christ as Lord.

So what do we do all week? We bear witness to Jesus Christ and to his present, living, reigning ministry of grace to Mrs. Smith, to the cancer patient in hospital, to the couple who come in to talk about getting married, to the parents anxious about the behavior of a teenage child, to the business owner whose small firm will not survive, to the young newly converted woman seeking baptism and to the family at the funeral scheduled for tomorrow. The one thing we must do is to speak of God, not generically but actually.

Everything else we might do is an addition to speaking of God. Because *God is* means *God acts,* we must speak of the God who has acted, does act and will act in time and space in, through and as Jesus Christ. Everything else we do is secondary, no matter what its seeming institutional, programmatic or administrative importance. Everything else we do takes its place as a result of the fact that we must speak concerning God in, through and as Jesus Christ.

The defining matter of the church's life is not to convert and bring people to faith (the evangelical heresy!) or to bring in the ethical commonwealth (the liberal heresy!). The defining matter for the church's life, for which the church exists, is to bear witness to Jesus Christ. He, not we, converts people and brings in the reign of God.

WHY WE HAVE SOMETHING TO DO

We have something to do only because the Lord Jesus shows up as a present, living and reigning Lord where actual people live and die—in living rooms, in hospital rooms, in divorce courts, in supermarkets, in classrooms, in automobiles or in movie theaters. The thing we must do is bear witness to the Lord who always gets there, wherever *there* is, ahead of us with his healing, saving, blessing, renewing, restoring, raising, forgiving, comforting and kingdom-bringing ministry of God's grace, love and communion.

When the Pharisees told Jesus to silence his disciples, Jesus responded, "I tell you, if these were silent, the stones would shout out" (Luke 19:40). The believers in Jerusalem prayed to speak the Word of God "with all boldness" (Acts 4:29) despite the judicial injunction "not to speak or teach at all in the name of Jesus" (Acts 4:18).

More Than Verbal

Preaching as bearing witness is more than a verbal act. Karl Barth famously invoked an image which summed up his theology. It was from Matthias Grunewald's rendering of the crucifixion in the centerpiece of the Isenheim altarpiece.

There is the tortured Christ on the cross. On his right Mary Magdalene kneels in prayer while the beloved disciple cradles Jesus' mother, Mary, in his arms. On his left stands John the Baptist with his extended, oversized index finger pointing to the Lord, directing the viewer's gaze away from himself to Jesus. Barth once commented that "It is this hand which is in evidence in the Bible." Near the hand in Latin are the words of John 3:30: "He must increase, but I must decrease." Says Barth, "Shall we dare turn our eyes in the direction of the pointing hand of Grunewald's John? We know whither it points. It points to Christ. But to Christ the crucified, we must immediately add. That is your direction, says the hand" (cited by Mangina in *Karl Barth: Theologian of Christian Witness* [Louisville, Ky.: Westminster/John Knox Press, 2004], p. 12).

We should note the other hands in the painting. There we can see the whole ministry of the church summed up. The primary direction is to look at the crucified Jesus. His enlarged hands show the agony of his atoning death for us. Then there are the enlarged praying hands of Mary Magdalene and the enlarged comforting hands of the apostle

John. The other hand of the Baptist holds the open Bible. Even the Lamb at the foot of the cross is holding the Communion cup into which its own blood is dripping.

JESUS, THE CONTENT OF FAITH

Bearing witness to Jesus is central because Jesus is the content of Christian faith, not as abstract doctrine but as a present, living and acting Lord in the freedom of his love and in the power of the Spirit. Our job is to bear witness not only to the past ministry of our Lord but also to his contemporaneous presence and act and to the horizon of promise and hope that his parousia opens up for us.

Ministry has a preeminent and existentially kerygmatic aspect. The gospel, Jesus Christ present now for the congregation or for the person before us, is to be proclaimed in some manner. No matter in what aspect, ministry always involves the proclamation of the real presence of Jesus Christ "the same yesterday and today and forever" (Hebrews 13:8).

Once this point is granted, the immediate concern is to discern what Jesus is up to in the particular circumstance or event or person with which we have to deal and bear witness to that in a manner appropriate to the issues and/or persons before us. More formally, we try to discern which aspects of his continuing ministry are the gospel in this circumstance or for this person now and bear witness to it.

THE DECLARATIVE MOMENT

Look for and anticipate the declarative moment when you will bear witness to Jesus Christ as the principal actor in the pastoral environment. The manner and timing of this moment are matters of pastoral discernment and giftedness, the fruit of our union with Christ. Discernment is what we should pray for and prepare for as we approach a pastoral event. The minister should expect to attest to the gospel by bearing witness to Jesus Christ in some specific aspect of who he is for that person or in that situation.

Declarative does not mean *didactic*. Most likely an impenitent man will not be argued into repentance, or a dying parishioner talked into hope or an aggrieved spouse debated into forgiveness. Pastoral ministry is rarely an occasion for an argument. Instead we speak an announcement of the gospel in some regard.

Here are brief examples of what I mean:

- "Christ offers you his forgiveness, even now. Let's talk about repentance and amendment of life."
- "Your future is in the hands of the Lord who loved you from the foundation of the world, and he will not ever let you go."
- "You may have given up on yourself, but Jesus has not given up on you!"
- "The Lord Jesus is present with you now in your pain and fear. His word to you is that whether you live or die, nothing will ever separate you from his love."
- "Your father has died and risen with Christ."

In pastoral work we are concerned with the gospel preached in the sermon and celebrated in the sacraments, now witnessed to privately and personally. The same gospel, Jesus Christ, who is attested in worship is now attested to the individual. We bear witness to some aspect of the ministry of Jesus Christ that we prayerfully believe and trust is the content of God's ministry to and for that person at this hour, in this place, in this condition of life.

We trust that in the freedom of his love and in the power of the Spirit, Jesus has here and now a dual ministry. (1) He has drawn near to the person to bless or to heal, to comfort or to encourage, to admonish or to direct, to forgive or to correct and so on. (2) He enables us to participate in his ministry for this person by bearing witness to his presence and work.

INTERPRETING THE LIFE SITUATION

Here we enter the pastoral conversation proper. Pastoral care as a sharing in the ministry of the grace of God assumes now a hermeneutical perspective. We think especially and specifically of helping that person to interpret his or her life situation in the light of the fact that Jesus Christ lived and died for this person who therefore has been forgiven and restored to fellowship with the Father.

In Jesus Christ this person has been elected to be God's friend and is now called through the Holy Spirit to live this truth. God has really acted in this person's life and his/her situation has been altered from enmity toward God to peace with God. In baptism this person has died to sin to "walk in newness of life" (Romans 6:4). Now matter how the person before us is constituted physically, psychologically and sociologically, that which the person *is*, not in a theoretical or merely spiritual or psychological sense but actually, is that he or she is forgiven and restored to communion with God.

In a manner similar to bearing witness, the hermeneutical work of interpretation will reflect various appropriate aspects of the gospel. Some occasions will easily lend themselves to interpretation in the light of the gospel, such as baptism preparation, sickness and death, funerals, salvation concerns, moral crises, marriage commitments and family concerns. Others may not so readily be brought under the light of Jesus Christ, such business concerns or success or failure on the sports field. The hermeneutical aspect of the pastoral work means that as appropriate, and in the right time, the pastoral conversation will seek to allow and enable a person to examine and reflect on his or her life circumstance in the light of the gospel, to gain deeper insight into the truth of his or her life in Christ as it touches this presenting life event.

We do not simply lay the gospel alongside a person, bearing witness to Jesus Christ, trusting that he is up to something. Instead we take time to allow the person to discover how the gospel discloses his or her life in a new way, leading to deeper understanding, changed perspective and more faithful discipleship. We must invite and enable a conversation in which a parishioner's story and the gospel story interpenetrate one another so that deeper understanding of a life situation occurs in terms of Jesus Christ.

Wait for the Right Time

Not every situation which confronts us will immediately call for interpretation. A certain amount of leisure, reflective energy and commitment to a process of conversation is required. The goal is not psychotherapy, valuable as that can be. The goal is directly related to a person's ongoing formation in Christ, to serious considerations of amendment of life or to deepened discipleship.

Always we operate trusting that Jesus Christ is present between parishioner and minister. He is the third actor in the conversation. He has a gospel-goal for the parishioner, which we jointly seek to discern. The task of pastoral interpretation is through and through theological, always asking the key question Who is Jesus Christ for this person, and what does this mean for faith and faithfulness?

Symbolic Action

During my hospitalization following cancer surgery, many ministers made visits. Some prayed with me, a few read Scripture, but none anointed me with oil or engaged in brief liturgical acts attesting forgiveness of sin or offered to celebrate holy Communion.

I am very grateful for the warmth of the affection these visits indicated and for the piety expressed. In fact I am grateful beyond telling and do not intend personal criticism. I merely observe how far Protestant pastoral care has moved away from seeing worship close to the center of its work or from understanding the pastoral use of the symbols of the faith.

During those long and difficult days my most profound pastoral experience became my wife and me, at her insistence, reading Morning Prayer and Compline together. These times became the anchor of my days. They gave me a context within which to reflect on my illness and a sure sense of hope.

Especially lost to mainstream Protestantism is the liturgical rhythm of the classical daily liturgies, the reading of the daily lectionary and the singing of the great canticles of the faith such as the *Venite, Jubilate* and *Te Deum Laudamus*. Lost also is the glorious comfort of Compline at day's end and of the repeated Antiphon of assurance: "Guide us waking, O Lord, and guard us sleeping; that awake we may watch with Christ, and asleep we may rest in peace." I have a hunch that many of my Presbyterian brothers and sisters in ministry simply do not know this material exists, and if they did, they would not know what to do with it.

BEYOND DECLARATION AND INTERPRETATION

Pastoral work is expressed beyond declaration and interpretation. It moves on to gather up the pastoral event in action filled with symbolic power. The action may be as simple as saying a prayer, holding a hand or making the sign of the cross. It may be as complex as a home Eucharist, an anointing with oil or a private *viaticum*, a service of forgiveness and assurance for the dying. We are more than cognitive beings. We also live by evocative metaphors and acted-out symbols. Rightly know your way around the Psalter, but follow the Psalter's appreciation of the oil of blessing, and never leave home without a vial of oil prayed over to be an instrument of God's blessing. Always be prepared to read Scripture and to pray, but know that we don't bid Christ into the hospital room; he is already there. Rather let your prayers be oriented toward thanksgiving for blessings given and expected.

There is no condition that we can fulfill in order for our Lord to be present in grace. It is his promise and choice to be present in the freedom of his love and in the power of the Spirit. Consider the place of appropriate touch. Remember that the sign of the cross is the sign of salvation in Christ. John Knox of Edinburgh considered holy Communion to be a godly medicine for sick souls. Reflect on what role the sacrament may have as a healing and converting ordinance. In other words, what can you *do in act* to communicate to someone that he or she is blessed by God, beyond telling the person that he or she is blessed?

Benediction

I END EVERY CLASS—both lectures and seminars—with a benediction. A benediction is a declarative affirmation that the recipients are indeed held in the grace of the Lord Jesus Christ, the love of God and in the communion of the Holy Spirit. There is no "iffiness" about it. A benediction also reminds us that our theology is the offering of our minds to God as an act of worship. Allow me to continue that pattern here.

First, though, a brief preamble: Friends, I know ministry is hard. The pressures are heavy to bear. Often we feel trapped by our limits, and with respect to the things of God we are indeed limited in understanding and faithfulness. That's why we need a Savior. Many of us have worked diligently to become professionally competent. However, in spite of our good intentions, efforts and hopes for ministry, we are perhaps aware of a deep weariness, of sadness even, and joy in ministry is remembered as a long-ago, wistful anticipation that has never quite been fulfilled.

This book has been my own working through of the impossibility of *my* ministry, and, indeed, of its necessary crucifixion when I have put it at the center of things. It has taken me into my sixtieth year to begin to internalize some of the implications of Paul's injunction that I have been crucified with Christ and that it is no longer I who live but

Christ who lives in me (Galatians 2:19-20). This injunction is true in every aspect of Christian life, including my ministry. This alone is now my joy and my hope. Of course, I have not yet fully attained the goal of internalizing this, but I press on because Christ Jesus has made me his own (Philippians 2:12). I trust that to be true, even when I don't feel it.

I have offered these reflections to you with love and respect, trusting that Christ Jesus has made you his own and praying that

> according to the riches of his glory, [the Father] may grant that you may be strengthened in your inner being with power through his Spirit, and that Christ may dwell in your hearts through faith as you are being rooted and grounded in love. I pray that you may have the power to comprehend, with all the saints, what is the breadth and length and height and depth, and to know the love of Christ that surpasses knowledge, so that you may be filled with all the fullness of God. (Ephesians 3:16-19)

God bless you, my brothers and sisters in ministry.

Andrew Purves
Lent 2007

Case Studies for Reflection

When I teach this material in the seminary, I try to help students get inside bearing witness, interpretation and symbolic action by using a series of case studies. As students work through these pastoral scenarios they *try on* bearing witness, interpretation and symbolic action. Case studies allow them to experience these activities in a safe and reflective environment.

The following three case studies are aids for reflection rather than normative guides. Each case includes some basis in fact and much fiction. The cases move from less complex to more complex.

In the first case study, context defines the problem. The second plunges us deeply into the interface between doctrine and ministry at the point of family crisis where there is hardly any time to think the issues through. The third invites reflection on the care of the congregation amid sharp political division and acrimony.

I have found that these case studies work best when small groups wrestle through them together. Each small group tends to report back very different responses. Often the second and third case studies stimulate significant tension and even anger. Differences of theological opinion come into sharp relief.

Theological discernment of the presence of the living, acting and reigning Lord Jesus is very demanding work. In real life, it is in such thorny contexts and complex issues that we trust ourselves to the ministry of Jesus Christ in which he joins us to himself, seeking thus to bear witness to him, help people interpret their lives in terms of him and act symbolically to represent him. Engaged reflectively in the practice of ministry as theological praxis, our discernment of the presence of the living, acting Lord becomes itself an experience of theological astonishment that gladdens our hearts and brings deep joy to ministry even in the direst of circumstances.

Of course there is no cookie cutter pattern for this ministry. It involves the development of a christological hermeneutic which cannot be reduced to a single response. So there is no single right answer.

Case Study 1: Am I a Caring Professional?

The local high school has a monthly job fair for seniors. Professionals from related fields are invited to share with students the nature of their work, academic requirements, career prospects and so on. As a minister you have been invited to participate in a Caring Professions roundtable at the high school job fair. With you are a physician, a social worker, a psychologist and a community development activist. Each of you is asked to make a five-minute presentation on "caring as the work of my profession."

Consider these questions:

Are you a caring professional?
Is pastoral *care* a legitimate naming of what you do?
What does *pastoral* mean?

What is caring about pastoral care that is similar to or quite different from what your copresenters do in their caring? (It is possible that some of them are Christians.)

- Your colleagues at the round table are each developing specific skills. What specific skills do you bring?

- In view of their medical, counseling, social work and community expertise, how are you anything less than an amateur?
- Worship leadership aside for now, what is your job description?
- To what extent do you have to make a theological statement in order to meet the assignment?

COMMENTARY

Pastoral identity is not just a professional disposition to care for people. It is primarily an expression of faith and the response to the call of God. Because of the kerygmatic nature of ministry, the minister's caring is not turned back on himself or herself. Pastoral care is not primarily about the minister's care. Neither is the minister a professional for hire who is paid to care. His or her primary mission is to bear witness to Jesus Christ. The specific skill that is brought is theological rather than functional. Faithfulness means, then, that the minister must speak in the name of Jesus Christ, even in the high school.

CASE STUDY 2: A DEAD BABY: WHAT AM I SUPPOSED TO DO?

Jean and Bill are in their late thirties and have wanted a baby for a long time. They are loyal and faithful members of the congregation of which you are minister. Jean is seven months pregnant.

You receive a telephone call in the middle of the night from Bill. His wife, Jean, is in great distress and they are on their way to the emergency room. You have a brief muddled conversation; Bill is driving and not fully coherent. You are frantically thinking what you should do. You decide to go to the hospital. You operate on the assumption that if balanced people call you in the middle of the night, the situation must be urgent, maybe life or death. You get to the hospital and make your way to the obstetrics department to find Bill in the waiting room in tears.

You ask, "What happened?"

"The baby died. They're cleaning up Jean right now." Bill glances at his watch. "We'll get in, in a minute."

"I am so sorry."

"We want you to baptize the baby before they take him away."

How do you respond to Bill? What do you do? You have about one minute to decide!

A nurse arrives shortly; Jean can see you now. Jean is *very* upset. She is lying in bed, rigid, the covers pulled up tightly to her neck. The dead baby is wrapped in a sheet in a crib by the side of her bed. What is the nature of your ministry with Jean? With Bill? With the dead baby?

Pastoral care consists of

- bearing witness—in this situation, to what?
- interpretation—in this situation, of what?
- symbolic action—in this situation, doing what?

Commentary

All kinds of useful expressions of sympathy and functional advice are no doubt appropriate and necessary. The ministerial imperative, however, goes beyond these. What is the nature of theological praxis in this immediate specific context? Who is Jesus Christ for this couple on this tragic early morning?

Pastoral wisdom warns us against two dangers: banal theological clichés and folksy advice trying to ameliorate the present pain. The less said here the better. In this situation bearing witness to Jesus Christ will probably take the form of lived-out action filled with symbolic power to communicate the reality of the ministry of the present

Lord Jesus Christ. Baptism aside for now, the minister should encourage the father to lift the baby and take the child to the mother.

Now what to do? Our task is to find an answer to the question What is Jesus doing now? My thinking turns to the ministry of the ascended Christ. (1) The ascended Christ prays for us. That awareness would help me to stay calm. I know that Bill, Jean and their baby, as well as I, are all being prayed for. (2) The ascended Christ sends us the Holy Spirit as the present form of his presence. We are not alone. We are not powerless. Jesus is at work. (3) The ascended Christ presents us in his own name, for his own sake, to the Father.

Let me suggest that the primary pastoral task in this case is to bear witness to the third act of the ascended Christ: he presents us to the Father. At some point I would take the baby and say a very few words about what I am doing, such as "I am about to show you what Jesus is doing, right now, with your baby." I would then lift the baby upward with my arms extended and say something like this: "Father, I give you this child, in my name." I would tell Bill and Jean that Jesus has given the baby to the Father, who has received the child into his bosom. I might at that point conduct a very brief baptism-like liturgy to seal the ministry of the ascended Jesus in the minds of Jean and Bill.

I would encourage Bill and Jean to think about a funeral and would offer appropriate guidance.

Later there will be time for interpretation as with Bill and Jean we struggle with Why? questions and try to understand how God's story of love and redemption fits in with tragic death and loss. There too we will rely on the Paraclete, the Comforter, and not be quick to rush in with ostensible answers to questions that may be too hard yet to ask.

Case Study 3: The Power of the Flag

On national holidays the church member who serves as the church custodian plants small American flags in the front of the churchyard adjacent to the main street. The minister has repeatedly asked him not to do that. But as each significant national day comes around, he expresses his patriotic desire once again. The situation has become tense between this church member and the minister.

The minister holds this position:

- The church is independent of the state and the government.
- The church's allegiance is wholly and singularly to Jesus Christ.
- The national flag is a symbol, indeed an icon, of the nation and not of Christian faith.
- The placement of a non-Christian symbol in the churchyard represents a blurring of identities.

The church member brought the matter to the church board in order that a policy might be established. Needless to say, the matter was soon a subject of whispered congregational conversation. The minister met with the church member privately prior to the board meeting to explain the reasons for not flying the flag in the churchyard. At this visit, assurance was given that this family would continue to be provided with pastoral care and shown Christian love and respect. Opinions were again given and received by both sides.

The minister sought to empower the board to deal with the issue by way of guided reflections on Christian identity, Bible study and a season of focused prayer. The minister was firm in leadership, as likewise was the church member in presenting the alternative perspective. The board sided with the minister.

Following the vote, two symbolic acts have helped to restore the relationship between the church member and the minister and keep the congregation from dissension. The corporate confession of sin each week, with the declaration of pardon, and a congregation-wide passing of the peace allowed the parties to greet one another in Christ's mercy. The celebration of holy Communion, especially when the minister served the church member by intinction, was a powerful act of Christian unity.

- How would you handle the issue? And why?
- What are the theological grounds?
- Given what you decide, how are you bearing witness to Jesus Christ?
- What role would interpretation play in your process?
- What symbolic actions would you employ with the church member and with the congregation?

COMMENTARY

The American flag, indeed any flag, is more than an empty symbol. It is an icon of the country. It directs attention through itself to something greater, which the flag represents. The Eastern Church especially uses icons that are carefully and prayerfully drawn to focus the attention of the worshipers through the picture to the unpicturable God. In its uncanny ability to represent more than is in the picture, an icon is more than a symbol.

A national flag is an icon of the country it represents. That is why it is appropriately flown from government buildings, in civic institutions and in the military. It points to deep values and shared traditions. It represents ownership of a common history and a given identity. The flag stands for the nation. It has extraordinary evocative power.

But there is a danger with icons. They invite worship. Sometimes the icon itself becomes an object of worship rather than a conduit which directs worship onward to God. Protestants especially are very sensitive to this danger. An icon that becomes an object of worship is an idol.

National flags present a similar possible danger especially when placed in the context of a church. One might naturally assume that worship is an appropriate response to an icon displayed in a church context. When the icon is a national flag, there is a double danger. Either the flag or the nation becomes the object of worship. As Christians we worship only God through Jesus Christ. We do not confuse God and country.

The church does have its own powerful symbol which functions like an icon. It is unambiguous in its power to point to redemption in Jesus Christ. Our icon is the cross. If we are going to display anything in public, it should be the cross. This invites worship of the One who alone is worthy of worship.

This account is placed in the context of the start of the second Iraq war. I think the minister did well by firmly but lovingly helping the church member and the congregation over a very difficult hurdle by bearing witness to Jesus Christ. In this case it was not in sermon or public proclamation. Rather, it was in more intimate contexts where church members gathered to hear the minister's perspective. Emphasis was placed on interpretation and conversation, some of which proved to be very fruitful. To those less inclined to that route, symbolic action was the preferred route to take, especially in the context of worship where broken relationship slowly moved toward healing.

Name Index

Scripture Index